Aquinas
A Beginner's Guide

ONEWORLD BEGINNER'S GUIDES combine an original, inventive, and engaging approach with expert analysis on subjects ranging from art and history to religion and politics, and everything in-between. Innovative and affordable, books in the series are perfect for anyone curious about the way the world works and the big ideas of our time.

aesthetics
africa
american politics
anarchism
ancient philosophy
animal behaviour
anthropology
anti-capitalism
aquinas
archaeology
art
artificial intelligence
the baha'i faith
the beat generation
the bible
biodiversity
bioterror & biowarfare
the brain
british politics
the Buddha
cancer
censorship
christianity
civil liberties
classical music
climate change
cloning
the cold war
conservation
crimes against humanity
criminal psychology
critical thinking
the crusades
daoism
democracy
descartes
dewey
dyslexia
economics
energy
engineering

the english civil wars
the enlightenment
epistemology
ethics
the european union
evolution
evolutionary psychology
existentialism
fair trade
feminism
forensic science
french literature
the french revolution
genetics
global terrorism
hinduism
history
the history of medicine
history of science
homer
humanism
huxley
international relations
iran
islamic philosophy
the islamic veil
jazz
journalism
judaism
justice
lacan
life in the universe
literary theory
machiavelli
mafia & organized crime
magic
marx
medieval philosophy
the middle east
modern slavery
NATO

the new testament
nietzsche
nineteenth-century art
the northern ireland conflict
nutrition
oil
opera
the palestine–israeli conflict
parapsychology
particle physics
paul
philosophy
philosophy of mind
philosophy of religion
philosophy of science
planet earth
postmodernism
psychology
quantum physics
the qur'an
racism
rawls
reductionism
religion
renaissance art
the roman empire
the russian revolution
shakespeare
shi'i islam
the small arms trade
stalin
sufism
the torah
the united nations
the victorians
volcanoes
the world trade organization
war
world war II

Beginners
GUIDES

Aquinas
A Beginner's Guide

Edward Feser

ONEWORLD

A Oneworld Book

Published by Oneworld Publications 2009
Reprinted 2010, 2013, 2015, 2017, 2018, 2019, 2020, 2021, 2023

ISBN 978-1-85168-690-2
eISBN 978-1-78074-006-5

Typeset by Jayvee, Trivandrum, India
Cover design by Simon McFadden
Printed and bound in Great Britain by Clays Ltd, Elcograf S.p.A.

Oneworld Publications
10 Bloomsbury Street
London WC1B 3SR
England

Stay up to date with the latest books,
special offers, and exclusive content from
Oneworld with our newsletter

Sign up on our website
www.oneworld-publications.com

MIX
Paper from
responsible sources
FSC® C018072

Contents

Acknowledgements   vi

System of citations   vii

1 St. Thomas   1

2 Metaphysics   8

3 Natural Theology   62

4 Psychology   131

5 Ethics   174

Further reading   193

Index   200

Acknowledgements

For useful comments on an earlier draft of this book, I thank Christopher Kaczor, my editor Mike Harpley, and an anonymous referee. As always, I thank my beloved wife Rachel and our dear children Benedict, Gemma, Kilian, and Helena for their patience and love. Special thanks are owed to my father, Edward A. Feser, who advised me over twenty years ago that I ought to read Aquinas. You were right, Dad; I wish I had listened to you sooner. I dedicate this book to you.

System of citations

Listed below are the abbreviations used for works of Thomas Aquinas quoted or cited in the text. Unless otherwise indicated within the text, quotations are taken from the translations cited here.

CT   *Compendium theologiae*. Translated by Cyril Vollert as *Light of Faith: The Compendium of Theology* (Sophia Institute Press, 1993). References are by part and section number.

DEE   *De ente et essentia*. Translated by Robert P. Goodwin as "On Being and Essence," in Robert P. Goodwin, ed., *Selected Writings of St. Thomas Aquinas* (Prentice-Hall, 1965). References are by chapter.

DPN   *De principiis naturae*. Translated by Robert P. Goodwin as "The Principles of Nature," in Robert P. Goodwin, ed., *Selected Writings of St. Thomas Aquinas* (Prentice-Hall, 1965). References are by chapter and paragraph number.

In I Cor   *Super Epistolam Primam Pauli Apostoli ad Corinthios*. Commentary on St. Paul's first letter to the Corinthians, excerpt translated by Timothy McDermott in Timothy McDermott, ed., *Thomas Aquinas, Selected Philosophical Writings* (Oxford University Press, 1993).

In DA   *Sententia super De anima*. Translated by Kenelm Foster and Silvester Humphries as *Commentary on*

Aristotle's De Anima (Dumb Ox Books, 1994). References are by book, lecture number, and paragraph number.

In DC   *Sententia de caelo et mundo*. Translated by Fabian R. Larcher and Pierre H. Conway as *Exposition of Aristotle's Treatise On the Heavens*, in two volumes (College of St. Mary of the Springs, 1964). References are by book and lecture number.

In DH   *Expositio in librum Boethii De hebdomadibus*. Translated by Ralph McInerny as "How are Things Good? Exposition of On the Hebdomads of Boethius," in Ralph McInerny, ed., *Thomas Aquinas, Selected Writings* (Penguin Books, 1998).

In Meta   *Sententia super Metaphysicam*. Translated by John P. Rowan as *Commentary on Aristotle's Metaphysics* (Dumb Ox Books, 1995). References are by book, lesson number, and paragraph number.

In NE   *Sententia libri Ethicorum*. Translated by C. J. Litzinger as *Commentary on Aristotle's Nicomachean Ethics* (Dumb Ox Books, 1993). References are by book, lecture number, and paragraph number.

In PA   *Sententia super Posteriora Analytica*. Translated by Richard Berquist as *Commentary on Aristotle's Posterior Analytics* (Dumb Ox Books, 2007). References are by book and section number.

In Phys   *Sententia super Physicam*. Translated by Richard J. Blackwell, Richard J. Spath, and W. Edmund Thirlkel as *Commentary on Aristotle's Physics* (Dumb Ox Books, 1999). References are by book, lecture number, and section number.

QDA   *Quaestiones disputatae de anima*. Translated by John Patrick Rowan as *The Soul* (B. Herder, 1949). References are by article number.

QDM   *Quaestiones disputatae de malo*. Translated by Richard

Regan as *On Evil*, ed. Brian Davies (Oxford University Press, 2003). References are by question number and article number.

QDP   *Quaestiones disputatae de potentia Dei*. Translated by Lawrence Shapcote as *On the Power of God* (Newman Press, 1932; reprinted by Wipf and Stock, 2004). References are by question number and article number.

QDV   *Quaestiones disputatae de veritate*. Translated by Robert W. Mulligan, James V. McGlynn, and Robert W. Schmidt as *Truth*, in three volumes (Henry Regnery Company, 1954; reprinted by Hackett Publishing Company, 1994). References are by question number and article number.

SCG   *Summa contra gentiles*. Translated by Anton C. Pegis, James F. Anderson, Vernon J. Bourke, and Charles J. O'Neil as *On the Truth of the Catholic Faith*, in five volumes (Doubleday, 1955–1957; reprinted as *Summa Contra Gentiles* by the University of Notre Dame Press, 1975). References are by book, chapter, and paragraph number.

SENT   *Scriptum super libros Sententiarum*. Commentary on the Sentences of Peter Lombard, excerpt translated by Timothy McDermott in Timothy McDermott, ed., *Thomas Aquinas, Selected Philosophical Writings* (Oxford University Press, 1993).

ST   *Summa theologiae*. Translated by the Fathers of the English Dominican Province as *The Summa Theologica*, in five volumes (Christian Classics, 1981). References are by part, question number, and article number.

1

St. Thomas

> If we want to study Aquinas we should pay him the compliment of treating as important what he thought of as important. To study Aquinas as Aquinas is a poor piece of flattery, since Aquinas cared very little for Aquinas, while he did care for God and for science.
>
> C. F. J. Martin, *Thomas Aquinas: God and Explanations*, p. 203.

One approach to the study of the history of philosophy is to situate the great thinkers of the past within the historical contexts in which they worked and determine what social, political, cultural, and philosophical circumstances influenced their ideas. This approach certainly has its value, especially insofar as it can help us correctly to understand what a philosopher meant in saying this or that. If pursued too single-mindedly, however, it can distract us from what the thinkers themselves considered important. The philosophers of the past did not write in order to reflect their times or to provide future historians with something to do. Their work was intended to point beyond itself to something else – to the *truth* about things – and what matters ultimately is whether they succeeded. As Aquinas himself once wrote, "the study of philosophy is not about knowing what individuals thought, but about the way things are" (*In DC* I.22). This is the point of the remark by Christopher Martin quoted above. The main value of studying what Aquinas or any other thinker said about God, science, or some other topic is to find out whether what he said is true, or at least likely to lead us closer to the truth. As Martin goes on to add, studying a thinker of the *past*, specifically, has value insofar as it can help us determine whether what we take for granted in the present is itself true:

> If we want to know about the existence of God, or about the nature of science, we should read Aquinas, not merely the writers of this century ... The great benefit to be derived from reading pre-modern authors is to come to realise that after all we [moderns] might have been mistaken.

That Aquinas's work should be read as a challenge to us today – and a challenge, as we shall see, not merely to our conclusions, but to many of our premises too – is a central theme of this book. Whether one thinks that challenge ultimately succeeds or not, it is important to treat Aquinas as in this sense a living author rather than a museum piece.

Martin's reference to "science" might strike some readers as odd. Wasn't Aquinas a philosopher and a theologian, rather than a scientist? And given his concern with God and other matters of religion, weren't his opinions matters of faith rather than reason, scientific or otherwise? Yet the assumptions behind such questions are precisely the sort that Aquinas's philosophy challenges. For Aquinas, a science is an organized body of knowledge of both the facts about some area of study and of their causes or explanations (*In PA* I.4); and while this includes the fields typically regarded today as paradigmatically scientific (physics, biology, and so forth), it also includes metaphysics, ethics, and even theology. Furthermore, these latter sciences are as rational as the ones we are familiar with today. To be sure, a part of theology (what is generally called "revealed theology") is based on what Aquinas regards as truths that have been revealed to us by God. To that extent theology is based on faith. But "faith," for Aquinas, does not mean an irrational will to believe something for which there is no evidence. It is rather a matter of believing something on the basis of divine authority (*ST* II-

II.4.1), where the fact that it really has been revealed by God can be confirmed by the miracles performed by the one through whom God revealed it (*ST* II-II.2.9). In any case, there is another part of theology (known as "natural theology") that does not depend on faith, but rather concerns truths about God that can be known via reason alone. It is these purely philosophical arguments of natural theology with which we shall be concerned in this book, along with Aquinas's views in metaphysics, ethics, and psychology (which includes the study of the human mind, but extends well beyond this, as we will see).

Aquinas's life and works

Thomas was born circa 1225 at Roccasecca, near the town of Aquino in southern Italy, from which his aristocratic family derived its name (hence the sobriquet "Aquinas"). At five years old he was sent by his parents to be educated at the Benedictine Abbey at Monte Cassino, in the hope of setting him on the path to attaining, eventually, the prestigious position of Abbot. But while studying at Naples as a teenager, Aquinas came under the influence of the new Order of Friars Preachers, also known as the Dominicans after their founder St. Dominic. Attracted by its devotion to study and teaching, he joined the order at nineteen, much to the chagrin of his family, whose worldly ambitions for Thomas did not square with the Dominican life of poverty and simplicity. In the hope of getting him to change his mind, his brothers abducted him and put him under house arrest at the family castle at Roccasecca for about a year, though he spent the time committing to memory the entire Bible and the four books of the *Sentences* of Peter Lombard (a theological textbook then widely in use). Notoriously, they even went to the extent of sending a prostitute into his room on one occasion, but he chased her away with a flaming stick pulled from the fireplace, which he used afterward to make the sign of the cross on the wall. As the story has it, he then kneeled before the cross and prayed for the gift of perpetual chastity, which he received at the hands of two angels who girded his loins with a miraculous cord. Eventually his brothers relented and he was allowed to return to the Dominicans.

While a student at what would become the order's study center in Cologne, Aquinas acquired the unflattering nickname "the Dumb Ox" due to his taciturn character coupled with his considerable girth. The former trait owed largely to a humble unwillingness to call attention to himself, and despite his portliness it is said of Aquinas that he ate only once a day in order to devote himself more fully to his work. In any case, his genius became evident before long, leading his mentor Albert the Great (c. 1200–1280) famously to predict that the Ox's "bellowing" would someday be heard throughout the world.

The works of Aristotle (384–322 B.C.) had during the preceding century become once again available to scholars in the Latin West, which led to a renewed interest in his philosophy, and Albert was at the time the foremost thinker of this Aristotelian revival. Aquinas would go on to become an even more influential proponent of Aristotle, and was recommended by Albert in 1252 for a position as a lecturer at the University of Paris, where Aquinas was a great success. It was apparently during this time that he composed the short treatises *On the Principles of Nature* and *On Being and Essence*, which set out his core metaphysical ideas. This period also gave rise to the much longer treatment of disputed questions *On Truth*.

After 1259 Aquinas returned to Italy and produced the massive *Summa contra Gentiles*, a treatise devoted to defending the claims of orthodox Christianity against a wide variety of objections presented by Jews, Muslims, pagans, and heretics. Following this he began work on the even more massive (and never completed) *Summa Theologiae*, a systematic treatment of all the main issues of theology organized around the theme of how things ultimately derive from, and are destined to return to, God, their first cause and last end. Along the way it deals with a wide variety of topics in metaphysics, ethics, psychology, and other subjects. These two *Summae* are generally regarded as Aquinas's masterpieces. In the course of working on the second, he would also produce many other works, apparently intended in part as preliminary treatments of certain topics to be dealt with in the *Summa Theologiae*. These include treatises on disputed questions *On the Power of God* and *On the Soul* and a series of commentaries on the works of Aristotle.

This latter, commentarial project had another purpose as well, one to which Aquinas's eventual return to Paris may be related. The use of Aristotle's philosophy in expounding and defending Christian doctrine was highly controversial in Aquinas's day. Aristotle had taken several positions (such as the view that the universe had no beginning) that seemed incompatible with the claims of Christianity. So too had the followers of Averroes (1126–1198), the Muslim philosopher whose interpretation of Aristotle was regarded by many as authoritative. The Averroists had held, for example, that the human race shares a single intellect, which appears incompatible with the notion that each human being has an individual immortal soul. More traditional theologians thus regarded Aristotelianism as theologically dangerous, and preferred the Neoplatonic tradition in general, and Augustinianism in particular, as more suited to the needs of Christian theology. The controversy between defenders and critics of Aristotelianism was particularly fierce at the University of Paris, and Aquinas was determined to show that, when rightly understood, Aristotle's philosophy was not only compatible with Christianity, but the best means of expounding and defending it. In effect, he took a middle position between Averroism and Augustinianism, seeking to avoid the extremes of the former while showing that the key elements of the latter tradition could be incorporated into a broadly Aristotelian worldview. The result was a unique synthesis that has since come to be known as Thomism (after "Thomas," the name by which Aquinas was known during his lifetime).

In 1272 Aquinas returned once again to Italy. While saying Mass in Naples one day in 1273 he went into a trance, and appears to have had a mystical experience, after which he was unable to resume work on the *Summa Theologiae*. Famously, he explained that after what he had seen, everything he had written now seemed to him "like straw." Called to attend the Second Council of Lyons, he apparently hit his head against a low-lying tree branch while on the journey, and sustained a serious injury. He was taken to the Cistercian abbey at Fossanova, where he was nursed by the monks, but died on March 7, 1274.

In addition to his profound humility, the character traits for which Aquinas was most notable included a deep piety and an astounding capacity for sustained abstract thought. It is said of him that he was so single-minded in his devotion to God that he would leave the room when discussion turned away to some unrelated subject. He could become so absorbed in prayer or in a chain of philosophical or theological reasoning that he would sometimes forget where he was, fail to perceive the people around him, and even (as one account has it) fail to notice the flame from a candle he was holding as it burned his hand. According to another famous story, while at dinner with King Louis IX of France he got thinking about the Manichaean heresy, struck the table exclaiming "That settles the Manichees!" and called for his secretary to take down the argument that had just occurred to him. Suddenly realizing where he was, Aquinas apologized and explained to the other startled guests that he thought he was alone in his room. Related to this tendency towards abstraction appears to have been an extraordinary unflappability. Anscombe and Geach relate a story according to which Aquinas once came upon "a holy nun who used to be levitated in ecstasy." His reaction was to comment on how very large her feet were. "This made her come out of her ecstasy in indignation at his rudeness, whereupon he gently advised her to seek greater humility."

2
Metaphysics

Even among contemporary philosophers who are otherwise
unfamiliar with his work, it is fairly well known that Aquinas
held that the existence of God, the immortality of the soul, and
the content and binding force of the natural moral law could be
established through purely philosophical arguments (as opposed
to an appeal to divine revelation). But those arguments
themselves are in general very badly misunderstood by those
who are not experts on Aquinas. The reason is that most
contemporary philosophers have little or no awareness of just
how radically different the fundamental metaphysical assumptions of ancient and medieval philosophers are, in general, from
the assumptions typically made by the early modern philosophers and their successors. A distinctive conception of causation,
essence, form, matter, substance, attribute, and other basic
metaphysical notions underlies all of Aquinas's arguments in
philosophy of religion, philosophy of mind, and ethics; and it is
a conception very much at odds with the sorts of views one finds
in Descartes, Locke, Hume, Kant, and the other founders of
modern philosophy. While most contemporary philosophers
would probably not identify themselves as Cartesians, Lockeans,
Humeans, Kantians, or the like, their thinking about the
metaphysical concepts just noted nevertheless tends, however
unconsciously, to be confined within the narrow boundaries set
by these early modern thinkers. Hence when they come across
a philosopher like Aquinas, they unthinkingly read into his
arguments modern philosophical presuppositions he would have
rejected. The result is that the arguments are not only misinterpreted, but come across as far less interesting, plausible, and

defensible than they really are. In rejecting them, as contemporary philosophers tend to do, they do not realize that what they are rejecting is a mere distortion or caricature of Aquinas's position rather than the real McCoy.

An overview of Aquinas's general metaphysics is therefore a necessary preamble to a consideration of his views in these other areas of philosophy. Such an overview would be of value in any case, for Aquinas's metaphysical ideas are important and interesting in their own right. We shall also see that they are as defensible today as they ever were, and (ironically enough) that some work by contemporary philosophers, quite outside the camp of Thomists and otherwise unsympathetic to Aquinas's overall project, tends to support this judgment.

Act and potency

The Greek philosopher Parmenides (c. 515–450 B.C.) notoriously held that change is impossible. For a being could change only if caused to do so by something other than it. But the only thing other than being is non-being, and non-being, since it is just nothing, cannot cause anything. Hence, though the senses and common sense tell us that change occurs all the time, the intellect, in Parmenides' view, reveals to us that they are flatly mistaken.

The tendency of philosophers like Parmenides to pit the intellect against the senses and common sense is one that was firmly resisted by Aristotle. At the same time, Aristotle was loath simply to dismiss a theory like Parmenides' on the grounds that it was odd or counterintuitive; it was important to understand exactly *why* such a theory was mistaken. Aquinas, who (as we have seen) esteemed Aristotle above all other philosophers, followed him in these attitudes, and also in his specific reply to Parmenides, which appealed to the distinction between *act and potency*.

Parmenides assumed that the only possible candidate for a source of change in a being is non-being or nothing, which (of course) is no source at all. Aristotle's reply was that this assumption is simply false. Take any object of our experience: a red rubber ball, for example. Among its features are the ways it actually is: solid, round, red, and bouncy. These are different aspects of its "being." There are also the ways it is not; for example, it is not a dog, or a car, or a computer. The ball's "dogginess" and so on, since they don't exist, are different kinds of "non-being." But in addition to these features, we can distinguish the various ways the ball *potentially* is: blue (if you paint it), soft and gooey (if you melt it), and so forth. So, being and non-being are not the only relevant factors here; there are also a thing's potentialities. Or, to use the traditional Scholastic jargon, in addition to the different ways in which a thing may be "in act" or actual, there are the various ways in which it may be "in potency" or potential. Here lies the key to understanding how change is possible. If the ball is to become soft and gooey, it can't be the actual gooeyness itself that causes this, since it doesn't yet exist. But that the gooeyness is non-existent is not (as Parmenides assumed) the end of the story, for a potential or potency for gooeyness *does* exist in the ball, and this, together with some external influence (such as heat) that actualizes that potential – or, as the Scholastics would put it, which reduces the potency to act – suffices to show how the change can occur. Change just is the realization of some potentiality; or as Aquinas puts it, "motion is the actuality of a being in potency" (*In Meta* IX.1.1770), where "motion" is to be understood here in the broad Aristotelian sense as including change in general and not just movement from one place to another.

So far this may sound fairly straightforward, but there is more to the distinction between act and potency than meets the eye. First of all, some contemporary analytic philosophers might object that a thing is "potentially" almost anything, so that

Aristotle's distinction is uninteresting. For example, it might be said by such philosophers that we can "conceive" of a "possible world" where rubber balls can bounce from here to the moon, or where they move by themselves and follow people around menacingly. But the potentialities Aristotle and Aquinas have in mind are ones rooted in a thing's nature as it actually exists, and do not include just anything it might "possibly" do in some expanded sense involving our powers of conception. Hence, while a rubber ball has the potential to be melted, it does not, in the Aristotelian sense, have the potential to bounce to the moon or to follow someone around all by itself.

Second, and as indicated already, though a thing's potencies are the key to understanding how it is possible for it to change, they are merely a necessary and not a sufficient condition for the actual occurrence of change. An additional, external factor is also required. Potential gooeyness (for example), precisely because it is merely potential, cannot actualize itself; only something else that is already actual (like heat) could do the job. Consider also that if a mere potency could make itself actual, there would be no way to explain why it does so at one time rather than another. The ball melts and becomes gooey when you heat it. Why did this potential gooeyness become actual at precisely that point? The obvious answer is that the heat was needed to actualize it. If the potency for gooeyness could have actualized itself, it would have happened already, since the potential was there already. So, as Aquinas says, "potency does not raise itself to act; it must be raised to act by something that is in act" (*SCG* I.16.3). This is the foundation of the famous Aristotelian–Thomistic principle that "whatever is moved is moved by another" (*In Phys* VII.2.891). (The principle is true, incidentally, even of animals, which seem at first glance to move or change themselves; for what this always amounts to is really just one part of the animal being changed by another part. A dog "moves itself" across a room, but only insofar as the potential for motion in the dog's legs is actualized by the flexing of the leg muscles, and their potential for being flexed is actualized by the firing of the motor neurons, and the potential for the motor neurons to fire is actualized by other neurons; and so on.)

Third, while act and potency are made intelligible to us in relation to each other, there is an asymmetry between them such that "absolutely speaking act is prior to potency" (*SCG* I.16.3). A potential is always a potential *for* a certain kind of actuality; for example, potential gooeyness is just the potential to be actually gooey. Furthermore, potency cannot exist on its own, but only in combination with act; hence there is no such thing as potential gooeyness existing all by itself, but only in something like an actual rubber ball. It is incoherent to speak of something as both existing and being purely potential, with no actuality whatsoever. But it is not incoherent to speak of something as being purely actual, with no potentiality at all. (Indeed, as we shall see, for Aquinas this is precisely what God is: *Actus Purus* or "Pure Act.") So, while for us to understand act and potency we need to contrast them with one another, in the real world outside the mind actuality can exist on its own while potentiality cannot.

As will become evident from the remainder of this chapter, the distinction between act and potency forms the basis of Aquinas's entire metaphysical system; and as will become equally evident by the end of this book, the repercussions of this fundamental distinction extend well beyond general metaphysics. It is not for nothing that the first of the famous Twenty Four Thomistic Theses has it that: "Potency and Act divide being in such a way that whatever is, is either pure act, or of necessity it is composed of potency and act as primary and intrinsic principles." (This echoes Aquinas's own assertion that "potency and act divide being and every kind of being" [*ST* I.77.1, as translated by Pegis in *Basic Writings of Saint Thomas Aquinas*].)

Hylemorphism

Given what has been said so far, Aquinas, following Aristotle, concludes that "in everything which is moved, there is some kind of composition to be found" (*ST* I.9.1), in particular a composition of act and potency. Perhaps slightly better known to modern readers is a related Aristotelian doctrine to the effect that the ordinary objects of our experience are composites of *form* and *matter* – a doctrine known as *hylemorphism* (sometimes spelled "hylomorphism") after the Greek words *hyle* ("matter") and *morphe* ("form"). For instance, the rubber ball of our example is composed of a certain kind of matter (namely rubber) and a certain kind of form (namely the form of a red, round, bouncy object). The matter by itself isn't the ball, for the rubber could take on the form of a doorstop, an eraser, or any number of other things. The form by itself isn't the ball either, for you can't bounce redness, roundness, or even bounciness down the hallway, these being mere abstractions. It is only the form and matter together that constitute the ball. The difference between the act/potency distinction and the form/matter distinction is one of generality. Anything compounded of form and matter is also compounded of act and potency, but there are compounds of act and potency that have no matter (namely angels, as we shall see later on). Being compounds of form and matter is the specific way in which the things of our everyday experience are capable of undergoing change.

Sometimes this change concerns some non-essential feature, as when a red ball is painted blue but remains a ball nonetheless. Sometimes it involves something essential, as when the ball is melted into a puddle of goo and thus no longer counts as a ball at all. Aquinas refers to the former sort of change as a change in *accidents*, and to the latter as a change in *substance*, and corresponding to each is a distinct kind of form: "What makes something exist substantially is called *substantial form*, and what

makes something exist accidentally is called *accidental form*"
(*DPN* 1.3). For a ball merely to change its color is for its matter
to lose one accidental form and take on another, while retaining
the substantial form of a ball and thus remaining the same
substance, namely a ball. For a ball to be melted into goo is for
its matter to lose one substantial form and take on another, thus
becoming a different kind of substance altogether, namely a
puddle of goo. Now the goo itself might be broken down into
more basic chemical components. But what that would involve
is the matter underlying the goo taking on yet different substantial forms. To be sure, Aquinas tells us that "what is in potency
to exist substantially is called *prime matter*" (*DPN* 1.2), or in other
words that we can distinguish between matter having no form
whatsoever ("prime matter") and the various substantial forms
that it has the potential to take on. But this distinction is for him
a purely conceptual one. In reality, however matter may be
transformed, it will always have some substantial form or other,
and thus count as a substance of some kind or other; strictly
speaking, "since all cognition and every definition are through
form, it follows that prime matter can be known or defined, not
of itself, but through the composite" (*DPN* 2.14). The notion of
prime matter is just the notion of something in pure potentiality with respect to having any kind of form, and thus with
respect to being any kind of thing at all. And as noted above,
what is *purely* potential has no actuality at all, and thus does not
exist at all.

As this indicates, hylemorphism is anything but a "reduction-
istic" metaphysical position (that is, one claiming that some
seemingly diverse or complex phenomena in reality consist of
"nothing but" some more uniform or simpler set of elements).
Certainly it is at odds with contemporary materialism; the suggestion that "matter is all that exists" becomes simply incoherent on
a hylemorphic conception of matter, since matter by itself without
anything else (including any form) would just be non-existent.

Furthermore, while the hylemorphist holds that the substances of our ordinary experience are composites of form and matter, form and matter themselves in turn cannot be understood except in relation to the whole substances of which they are components. Hence the hylemorphic account is holistic and in no sense a "reduction" of substances even to their form and matter together.

This also indicates that Aristotle's and Aquinas's conception of "form" is not the same as Plato's. On the hylemorphic analysis, considered apart from the substances that have them, form and matter are mere abstractions; there is no form of the ball apart from the matter that has that form, and no matter of the ball apart from the form that makes it a ball specifically. In particular, the form of a ball does not exist in a "Platonic heaven" of abstract objects outside time and space. All the same, Aristotle and Aquinas are, like Plato, realists about universals: when we grasp "humanity," "triangularity," and the like, what we grasp are not mere inventions of the human mind, but are grounded in the natures of real human beings, triangles, or what have you. (More on this later.) Moreover, while (contra Plato) no form exists apart from some particular individual substance that instantiates it, not every form exists in a *material* substance. There can be forms without matter, and thus *immaterial* substances – namely, for Aquinas, angels and postmortem human souls. (Again, more on this later.) This recapitulates an asymmetry noted earlier: just as act can exist without potency even though potency cannot exist without act, so too form can exist without matter even though matter cannot exist without form (*DEE* 4).

In any event, where form and matter are concerned, while they are implicated in the explanation of how things come to be and pass away, they are not themselves the sorts of things that come to be and pass away. As Aquinas argues,

> we should note that prime matter, and even form, are neither generated nor corrupted, inasmuch as every generation is from

something to something. That from which generation arises is
matter; that to which it proceeds is form. If, therefore, matter
and form were generated, there would have to be a matter of
matter and a form of form *ad infinitum*. Hence, properly speaking, only composites are generated. (*DPN* 2.15)

However, as we will see in the next chapter, this does not entail
that the existence of form and matter does not stand in need of
explanation.

The four causes

Speaking of explanation naturally leads us to that most famous of
Aristotelian metaphysical doctrines, that of the four causes –
material, formal, efficient, and final – a doctrine to which
Aquinas is fully committed (*DPN* 3.20). Return yet again to the
rubber ball of our example. The *material cause* or underlying stuff
the ball is made out of is rubber; its *formal cause*, or the form,
pattern, or structure it exhibits, comprises such features as its
sphericity, solidity, and bounciness. In other words, the material
and formal causes of a thing are just its matter and form, considered as two aspects of a complete explanation of it. Next we
have the *efficient cause*, that which actualizes a potency and
thereby brings something into being. In this case that would be
the actions of the workers and/or machines in the factory in
which the ball was made, as they molded the rubber into the
ball. Lastly we have the *final cause* or the end, goal, or purpose
of a thing, which in the case of the ball might be to provide
amusement to a child. In combination, these causes provide a
complete explanation of a thing. That doesn't mean that in the
case of the ball, for example, you would not have many more
questions about it, such as where the rubber came from or who
made the factory. But the answers to such questions will all be

just further instances of material, formal, efficient, and final causes.

The four causes are completely general, applying throughout the natural world and not just to human artifacts. Biological organs provide the most obvious examples. For instance, to understand what a heart is, you need to know its material cause, namely that it is made out of muscle tissue of a certain sort. But there are many muscles in the body that aren't hearts, so you also need to know its formal cause, and thus such things as that the muscle tissue is organized into ventricles, atria, and the like. Then there is the efficient cause, which in this case would be the biological processes that determined that certain embryonic cells would form into a heart rather than, say, a kidney or a brain. Finally there is the heart's final cause, namely that it serves the function of pumping blood.

But biological organs and processes are by no means the only sorts of natural phenomena that exhibit final causality, and it is a mistake to assume (as is often done) that to speak of final causes is simply another way of speaking about functions. All functions are instances of final causality, but not all final causality involves the having of a function, if by "function" we mean the sort of role a bodily organ plays in the life of an animal or the role a mechanical part plays in the operation of a machine. For the Aristotelian, final causality or teleology (to use a more modern expression) is evident wherever some natural object or process has a tendency to produce some particular effect or range of effects. A match, for example, reliably generates flame and heat when struck, and never (say) frost and cold, or the smell of lilacs, or thunder. It inherently "points to" or is "directed towards" *this* range of effects specifically, and in that way manifests just the sort of end- or goal-directedness characteristic of final causality, even though the match does not (unlike a heart or a carburetor) function as an organic part of a larger system. The same directedness towards a certain specific effect or range of effects is evident in all causes operative in the natural world. When Aristotelians say that final causality pervades the natural order, then, they are not making the implausible claim that everything has a function of the sort biological organs have, including piles of dirt, iron filings, and balls of lint. Rather, they are saying that goal-directedness exists wherever regular cause and effect patterns do.

Hence Aquinas says that "every agent acts for an end: otherwise one thing would not follow more than another from the action of the agent, unless it were by chance" (*ST* I.44.4). By "agent" he means not just thinking beings like us, but anything that brings about an effect. His point is that unless a cause were inherently directed towards a certain effect or range of effects – that is to say, unless that effect or range of effects were the cause's own final cause – there would be no reason *why* it should bring about just that effect or effects. In other words, we cannot make sense of efficient causality without final causality. They go hand in hand, just as a thing's material and formal causes go hand in hand in the sense that matter cannot exist without form and form, in the ordinary case anyway, does not exist without matter.

At the same time, just as form is ultimately prior to matter (and, more generally, act prior to potency), final causes are prior to or more fundamental than efficient causes, insofar as they make efficient causes intelligible (*DPN* 4.25). Indeed, for Aquinas the final cause is "the cause of causes" (*In Phys* II.5.186), that which determines *all* of the other causes. For something to be directed towards a certain end entails that it has a form appropriate to the realization of that end, and thus a material composition suitable for instantiating that form; a knife, for example, if it is to fulfill its function of cutting, must have a certain degree of sharpness and solidity, and thus be made of some material capable of maintaining that degree of sharpness and solidity. Thus the existence of final causes entails the existence of formal and material causes too. More generally, for something to have some feature potentially entails a kind of directedness to the actualization of that potential; as Aquinas puts it, "an ordering or tendency to an act belongs to a thing existing with a potency to that act" (*In Phys* III.2.285, as translated by Renard at p. 23 of his *Philosophy of Being*). Hence the existence of final causes also entails the act/potency distinction. Implicit within the notion of final causality, then, is the entire Aristotelian metaphysical apparatus.

It is important to understand (again, contrary to a common misconception) that most final causality is thought by Aristotelians to be totally unconscious. As Aquinas writes, "although every agent, be it natural or voluntary, intends an end, we should realize nevertheless that it does not follow that every agent knows or deliberates about the end" (*DPN* 3.19). The match is "directed towards" the production of fire and heat, the moon is "directed towards" movement around the earth, and so forth. But neither the match nor the moon is *aware* of these "goals." The match isn't thinking "I must generate heat," and the moon isn't thinking "I must go around the earth," for of course neither one is thinking anything at all. For Aristotelians, our conscious thought processes are only a special case of the more general phenomenon of goal-directedness or final causality, which exists in the natural world in a way that is mostly divorced from any conscious mind or intelligence. To "intend an end" in the sense Aquinas has in mind in the passage just quoted is not necessarily to make a conscious decision to pursue some goal, but rather just "to have a natural inclination toward something" (*DPN* 3.19). We intend an end like going to the supermarket after conscious deliberation, but the match "intends" the end of generating heat, the heart "intends" the end of circulating the blood, and the moon "intends" the end of moving around the earth, all in a totally unconscious and non-deliberative way.

As with final causes, the Aristotelian notion of efficient causality is very commonly misunderstood by contemporary readers. Of the four causes, it is sometimes said to be the one that most closely corresponds to modern philosophical notions of causation, but this is misleading at best. As has already been noted, for the Aristotelian, efficient causes cannot be understood apart from final causes, and yet modern philosophers (for reasons we will examine presently) tend to deny the very existence of final causes. This seems to be the reason why modern philosophers have, at least since David Hume (1711–1776), tended to think it "conceivable" that any cause might produce any effect or none. For example, when a brick is thrown towards a window, we naturally expect that the window will shatter, but (so it is said) it is at least in theory possible that the brick might instead turn into a bouquet of flowers, or disappear altogether. Causes and effects are, in Hume's words, "loose and separate," with no "necessary connection" holding between them. Hence (the Humean argument continues) it may be that it is only the "constant conjunction" of thrown bricks and shattered windows in our experience that leads us to expect the latter in the presence of the former. The necessity with which we think the one brings about the other may be merely a projection of this expectation, thus deriving from our subjective psychological tendencies rather than any objective feature of the causes and effects themselves. Aristotle and Aquinas would have found all of this unintelligible, in part because for them, nothing counts as an efficient cause in the first place unless it is inherently ordered towards the generation of a certain kind of effect or range of effects as its final cause. Humean analyses of causation, along with the philosophical puzzles they notoriously give rise to, are only possible if one rejects the Aristotelian notion of final causality, and thus the Aristotelian notion of efficient causality along with it.

Aristotle and Aquinas would also be baffled by the modern tendency to think of causation as essentially a relation between temporally ordered events, a tendency underlying the Humean assumption that it is at least "conceivable" that the thrown brick might result in something other than the broken window. The brick is thrown; that's one event. The window shatters; that's another event. Obviously the second event follows the first in time, and is therefore distinct from it. Hence it seems equally obvious that the one could in principle exist without the other, and thus (the modern philosopher concludes) that an effect might conceivably fail to follow upon its usual cause. But from the Aristotelian point of view, this is simply a wrongheaded way of characterizing the causal situation. For Aristotle and Aquinas, it is *things* that are causes, not events; and the immediate efficient cause of an effect is *simultaneous* with it, not temporally prior to it. "It should be understood in speaking of actual causes that what causes and what is caused must exist simultaneously, such that if the one exists, the other does also" (*DPN* 5.34). In the case of the broken window, the key point in the causal series would be something like the pushing of the brick into the glass and the glass's giving way. These events are simultaneous; indeed, the brick's pushing into the glass and the glass's giving way are really just the *same* event considered under different descriptions. Or (to take an example often used to illustrate the Aristotelian conception of efficient causation) we might think of a potter making a pot, where the potter's positioning his hand in just such-and-such a way and the pot's taking on such-and-such a shape are simultaneous, and, again, the same event described in two different ways. In examples like these, it is simply not plausible to suggest that the causes and effects are "loose and separate" or lack any "necessary connection." It is difficult to see how it is even "conceivable" that the brick's passing through the glass might not be accompanied by the glass's giving way, or that the hand's shaping the clay might occur without the clay's being shaped. The causes and effects themselves are distinct – the brick and its action are not the same as the glass and its reaction, and the position of the potter's hand is not the same as the pot's shape – but since they exist in one and the same event, there is no way to appeal to a distinction between events to motivate the claim that cause and effect might come apart. And when we consider the specific details of the immediate causal situation – speaking precisely, for example, of the brick's pushing through the glass and the glass's giving way, and not (more loosely) of thrown bricks being followed by broken windows – it is hard to see what it could mean to suggest that such a cause might not be followed by such an effect.

Famously, Hume also claims that something could in principle come into being without any efficient cause whatsoever. Aquinas would deny this, arguing, as we have seen he does, that "potency does not raise itself to act" and hence that "whatever is moved is moved by another," a thing's coming into existence just being an instance of motion or the actualization of a potency. More generally, "everything whose act of existing is other than its nature [must] have its act of existing from another" (*DEE* 4). In other words, whatever is contingent, not having its existence by virtue of its own nature, must be caused to exist by something else.

A corollary of this is that "effects must needs be proportionate to their causes and principles" (*ST* I-II.63.3) such that "whatever perfection exists in an effect must be found in the effective cause" (*ST* I.4.2). For a thing cannot give what it does not have. Sometimes what is in the effect exists in the cause in just the same way it exists in the effect; that is to say, "the form of the thing generated pre-exists in the generator according to the same mode of being and in a similar matter, as when fire generates fire or man begets man" (*In Meta* VII.8.1444). Sometimes it exists in the cause "neither according to the same mode of being, nor in a substance of the same kind" as when "the form of a house pre-exists ... in the mind of the builder" (*In Meta* VII.8.1445). Sometimes it is in the cause "more excellently, as, heat is in the sun more excellently than it is in fire" (*ST* I.6.2). And sometimes it is in the cause "virtually but not actually" as "when heat is caused by motion, heat is present in a sense in the motion itself as in an active power" or when "the form of numbness is in the eel which makes the hand numb" (*In Meta* VII.8.1448–9). Thus, to use the standard Scholastic jargon, even if the effect is not always contained in the cause "formally," it will yet be contained in it "eminently" or "virtually."

This last principle came to be known within the Scholastic tradition as the *principle of proportionate causality*. That whatever comes into existence, and more generally that any contingent thing, must have a cause, came to be known as the *principle of causality*. Aquinas's dictum that "every agent acts for an end" is known as the *principle of finality*. These three principles are central to Aquinas's general metaphysics, and, as we shall see in the next chapter, to his arguments concerning the existence and nature of God in particular. As our discussion thus far has implied, the principle of finality is in a sense the most fundamental of them, given that the final cause is "the cause of causes": for, again, in Aquinas's view an efficient cause can bring an effect into being only if it is "directed towards" that effect; and it is ultimately in that sense that the effect is "contained in" the efficient cause. Yet as I have said, modern philosophers tend to reject, and indeed even dismiss, the very notion of final causality; and (unsurprisingly, given this circumstance) they also tend to reject, or are at least suspicious of, the other two principles as well. However, it is by no means clear that there really are any good reasons for these attitudes, and the three principles are in any case eminently defensible. Before we see why, however, let us complete our survey of Aquinas's metaphysical framework by examining some of its components that most clearly constitute developments of Aristotelian ideas beyond the point at which Aristotle himself left them.

Essence and existence

We have seen that Aquinas, unlike Plato, does not regard the forms of things as existing independently of the individual substances they are the forms of, but also that he is nevertheless a realist about universals and that he thinks it possible for some forms to exist without matter. To understand these doctrines, we need now to look at Aquinas's famous theory of essence and its relationship to existence.

The essence of a thing is just that which makes it the sort of thing it is, "that through which something is a certain kind of being" (*DEE* 1). It is also that through which a thing is intelligible or capable of being grasped intellectually. Hence to grasp *humanity* is to grasp the essence of human beings – that which makes them human – and thus to understand what a human being is; to grasp *triangularity* is to grasp the essence of triangles – that which makes them triangles – and thus to understand what a triangle is; and so forth. A thing's essence is also sometimes called its "nature," "quiddity," or "form" (though as we shall see, "form" sometimes has a narrower sense in which it refers to only a part of a thing's essence). The doctrine that (at least some) things have real (as opposed to merely conventional) essences is called *essentialism*.

It is part of the essence of a triangle that it have three straight sides, but not part of the essence that it be drawn with blue, red, or any other particular color of ink. That is why a triangle remains a triangle whatever color it is, but cannot continue to exist if it loses one of its sides. This sort of consideration has led some contemporary analytic philosophers to think of the essence of a thing as definable in terms of whatever features it would exhibit in every possible world, where a "possible world" is a complete and logically consistent description of how things might have been. Triangles would have three sides in every possible world in which they exist at all, but would not be blue in every possible world in which they exist; and this (the theory in question says) is what it amounts to to say that three-sidedness is part of the essence of triangles and blueness is not.

It is important to emphasize that this contemporary form of essentialism, associated with philosophers like Saul Kripke and Hilary Putnam, is (as contemporary Thomists like David Oderberg and Gyula Klima have pointed out) very different from the Aristotelian form of essentialism adopted and developed by Aquinas. From an Aristotelian–Thomistic point of view, the possible worlds analysis of essence has things backwards: we need to know what the essence of a thing is first, before we can know what it would be like in various possible worlds; talk of possible worlds, if legitimate at all, must get explained in terms of essence, not essence in terms of possible worlds. Furthermore, the possible worlds analysis obliterates an important distinction much emphasized in Aristotelian essentialism. Consider Socrates' rationality and his ability to learn languages (to borrow an example from Christopher Shields). Socrates has these in every possible world in which he exists at all, and thus, the contemporary essentialist concludes, both features are essential to him. But from the Aristotelian point of view, Socrates' ability to learn languages, though one of his necessary features – for him to lose it would entail that he ceases to exist – is nevertheless not as basic to him as his rationality is. The reason is that his ability to learn languages *derives from* his rationality; its necessity, though real, is therefore a derived necessity. It is only those features of a thing that are not derived in this way that can, from the Aristotelian point of view, count as part of the essence of a thing. Those features deriving from the essence, such as Socrates' ability to learn languages, are instead referred to as "properties," since they are proper or necessary to a thing in a way that its purely contingent features (like Socrates' being in Athens or having been a soldier) are not. ("Property" thus has a different connotation in Aristotelian metaphysics than it does among most contemporary philosophers, who use it as more or less synonymous with what Aquinas would instead call an "accident," viz. that which exists only as an attribute of a substance, as e.g. redness exists only in red things.)

To say that *humanity* is that which makes all of us human beings implies that this essence is something *shared* by all human beings, that we all have the *same* essence; and in general, the essence of a thing is something it shares with others in the same kind. In this sense humanity constitutes a natural kind or species, namely the one traditionally defined as falling under the genus *animal* and as differentiated from other species in that genus by virtue of its members being *rational*. (More simply: human beings are by nature *rational animals*.) Thus considered, however, *humanity* exists, not in the world outside the mind, but as a concept. "The character *species* is included among the accidents which follow upon [an essence or nature] according as it exists in the intellect. The characters *genus* and *difference* also belong to nature so considered" (*DEE* 3). But Aquinas is by no means a conceptualist of the Lockean sort; he does not (as Locke later would) regard species as simply conventional or "made by men." Though *humanity* and the like qua universals exist only in the intellect, "such conceptions have an immediate basis in reality" (I *SENT* 2.1.3). To be sure, what is universal to human beings does not exist outside the mind apart from particular human beings themselves; Socrates' humanity, for example, does not exist in him apart from those of his features which he does not share with, and which distinguish him from, other human beings. But that doesn't entail that humanity does not exist *at all* in Socrates, George Bush, and other human beings, only that it does not exist in them in the abstract way in which it exists in the intellect, that is, divorced from all individualizing features. Aquinas is thus a realist, albeit of the Aristotelian or "moderate" sort (as opposed to the "extreme" realism represented by Plato's Theory of Forms). "The nature is said to be in the thing inasmuch as there is something in the thing outside the soul that corresponds to the conception of the soul" (I *SENT* 2.1.3, as translated by Pasnau and Shields at p. 78 of their *Philosophy of Aquinas*).

So, what is outside the mind is just human nature as it exists concretely in individual human beings: the humanity of Socrates, the humanity of George Bush, and so forth. What exists within the mind is humanity considered abstractly, as a universal that might be applied to many individuals. But humanity *as such* is neither particular nor universal, neither one nor many, and *could not* be either, for "each is extrinsic to the notion of humanity, and either can happen to it" (*DEE* 3). If universality or "manyness" was part of humanity as such, then humanity could never exist in a particular thing, as it obviously does in (for example) Socrates. If particularity or "oneness" was part of humanity as such, then humanity could never be shared by multiple distinct individuals, as it obviously is shared by (for example) Socrates and George Bush. Hence, "universals as such exist only in the soul; but the natures themselves, which are conceivable universally, exist in things" (*In DA* II.12.380).

With respect to material things, "the term 'essence' signifies the composite of matter and form" (*DEE* 2), and not just the form alone; "otherwise," Aquinas says, "there would be no difference between definitions in physics and in mathematics" (*DEE* 2). What he means is that when we understand what a material thing is, what we understand is different from the sort of thing we understand when studying geometry and the like, in that it is not a pure abstraction but something concrete. You can ignore the material structure of a particular circle, square, or triangle when learning a geometrical theorem, but you cannot ignore the material structure of particular rocks, trees, or animals when studying geology or biology. Hence matter is part of the essence of objects of the latter sort. At the same time, matter is for Aquinas the "principle of individuation" between members of a species of material things, that which makes them *distinct* things of the same type (*DEE* 2). So how can matter be part of the essence of trees (for example) – and thus common to all trees – and at the same time be that which distinguishes one tree from another? The answer is that we must make a distinction between matter in general, and this or that particular parcel of matter. It is the former, or "common matter," that is part of the essence of trees, and the latter, or "designated matter," that individuates one tree from another. All trees are material, but what makes this tree different from that one despite the fact that they have the same essence is that this one is composed of this particular hunk of matter, and that one is composed of that distinct particular hunk of matter.

With what Aquinas calls "separated substances" – that is to say, immaterial realities like the soul, angels, and God – things are not so straightforward. The soul, as we will see in chapter 4, must on Aquinas's view be conjoined to matter at some point in its existence, even if it can exist beyond the death of the body. There is accordingly no difficulty in principle in explaining how one soul can be individuated from another, even if this requires a qualification to the thesis that matter is the principle of individuation. God, as shall see below, is necessarily unique in any case, so that the question of individuation cannot arise. But what about angels, which are supposed to be both distinct from one another and yet completely immaterial? An angel, says Aquinas, is a form without matter, and thus its essence corresponds to its form alone (*DEE* 4). But precisely because there is no matter to distinguish one angel in a species from another, "among these substances there cannot be many individuals of the same species. Rather, there are as many species as there are individuals" (*DEE* 4).

Does this mean that an angel, as a pure form, is also pure actuality, devoid of potency? By no means. Even an angel has to be created, and thus pass from potency to act. But since angels are immaterial, this cannot involve matter taking on a certain form. What it does involve is the form or essence being conjoined to what Aquinas calls an *actus essendi* or "act of existing." Matter is "in potency" or only potential relative to form, which is what actualizes matter. But relative to the act of existing, both pure form (as in an angel) and a composite of form and matter (as in a material object) are themselves in potency or only potential. Hence even angels, like material things, are composites of act and potency insofar as they are composites of an essence with an act of existing (*DEE* 4).

Here we come at last to Aquinas's famous doctrine of the distinction between essence and existence. To return again to our example of humanity, "it is ... evident that the nature of man considered absolutely abstracts from every act of existing, but in such a way, however, that no act of existing is excluded by way of precision" (*DEE* 3). That is to say, there is nothing in our grasp of the essence *humanity* as such that could tell us whether or not any human beings actually exist, if we didn't already know they did. In general, "every essence or quiddity can be understood without its act of existing being understood. I can understand what a man or phoenix is, and yet not know whether or not it exists in the nature of things" (*DEE* 4). The phoenix example is perhaps more instructive than the humanity one: someone unaware that the phoenix is entirely mythical might know that its "essence" is to be a bird that burns itself into ashes out of which a new phoenix arises, without knowing whether there really is such a creature. But in that case, "it is evident that the act of existing is other than essence or quiddity" for "whatever is extraneous to the concept of an essence or quiddity is adventitious, and forms a composition with the essence" (*DEE* 4). Or in other words, if it is possible to understand the essence of a thing without knowing whether it exists, its act of existing (if it has one) must be distinct from its essence, as a metaphysically separate component of the thing.

The significance of the distinction between essence and existence is indicated by another argument Aquinas gives for it. If essence and existence were not distinct, they would be identical; and they could be identical only in "something whose quiddity is its very act of existing ... such that it would be subsistent existence itself" (*DEE* 4). That is to say, something whose essence is its existence would depend on nothing else (e.g. matter) for its existence, since it would just *be* existence or being. But there could only possibly be one such thing, for there would be no way in principle to distinguish more than one. We could not coherently appeal to some unique form one such thing has to distinguish it from others of its kind, "because then it would not be simply an act of existing, but an act of existing plus this certain form"; nor could we associate it with some particular parcel of matter, "because then it would not be subsistent existence, but material existence," that is, dependent on matter for its being (*DEE* 4). In fact there is, in Aquinas's view, a being in whom essence and existence are identical, namely God; and the identity of his essence and his existence entails (among other things) that God is a necessary being, one that cannot possibly not exist. But all of this shows that in everything other than God, essence and existence must be distinct. For in the case of material objects (for example) there is more than one member of each kind, and none of them exists in a necessary way but only contingently; and this would not be so if essence and existence were in these things identical.

We will have more to say about the theological implications of Aquinas's teaching on essence and existence in chapter 3. For now we can note that his conception of God as that in which essence and existence are identical dovetails nicely with the older Aristotelian notion of God as pure act. Indeed, the notion of angels as composites of form and an act of existence fits in naturally with the Aristotelian (though also neo-Platonic) idea of a hierarchy of being, extending from pure act at the top to prime

matter at the bottom, with greater degrees of potency characterizing each step down the ladder. Prime matter cannot exist on
its own precisely because it is pure potency. Material substances
can exist on their own because in addition to matter they have
form, and thus some degree of act. Human beings have a higher
degree of act and thus a lesser degree of potency, because (for
reasons we'll examine in chapter 4) their souls are subsistent,
capable of existing apart from the body. Angels, being devoid of
matter altogether, have a yet higher degree of act, though even
they fall short of the summit of reality, God, since unlike him
they are (as we saw earlier) still composites of potency and act.
Distinctions between the angels, even given that they are of
different species, are possible at all in Aquinas's view only insofar
as they too differ in degree of potency or act, in particular with
respect to an immaterial power like intelligence. Hence, "a
superior intelligence which is nearer to the first being would
have more act and less potency; and so on with the others. This
terminates in the human soul, which holds the lowest grade
among intellectual substances" (*DEE* 4).

The transcendentals

Aquinas, following Aristotle, regards metaphysics as the "science
which studies being as being," rather than (as other sciences do)
studying some one particular kind of being among others (*In
Meta* IV.1.529). (For this reason, metaphysicians in the
Thomistic tradition have often preferred the label "ontology" –
from the Greek *ontos* or "being" – as an apt name for their disci-
pline.) Act and potency, form and matter, essence and existence,
substance and accident, and the like are all merely aspects of
being, and their study gives us a greater understanding of it. Still,
strictly speaking, we cannot define being the way we can define
a species like *humanity*, by citing a genus it falls under and a

specific difference that marks it off from other species in the genus. Being is the most comprehensive concept we have, applying as it does to everything that exists, so that there is no way to subsume it under something more general. Moreover, being cannot even properly be regarded as a genus under which everything else falls, for any genus can be "added to" in a way being cannot. For example, under the genus *animal* we can distinguish the species *vertebrate* and *invertebrate*. (Here we are using "genus" and "species" in the logical sense, not the modern biological sense.) But precisely since *animal* includes both vertebrates and invertebrates, it is not *itself* either vertebrate or invertebrate; for it cannot itself be *both* (on pain of contradiction), and if it was one rather than the other, it would not be able to include the other as a species. Hence to get the concept of either *vertebrate* or *invertebrate*, we need to add something to the concept *animal*. By contrast, says Aquinas, "nothing can be added to being as though it were something not included in being – in the way that a difference is added to a genus or an accident to a subject – for every reality is essentially a being" (*QDV* 1.1).

Thus, though "being" is not an *equivocal* term – unlike "dog" as applied to an animal and to a constellation, we do not call different things "beings" in senses which are completely different – neither is it a *univocal* term, since its application is so absolutely general that not all the things it applies to can possibly be considered "beings" in exactly the same sense. Being is instead what Aquinas would call an *analogical* notion, where analogy constitutes a middle ground between the equivocal and univocal usage of terms (*In Meta* XI.3.2197). For example, accidents and substances can both be said to have being, but accidents lack the independent existence that substances have; material things and angels can both be said to have being, but material things are composites of matter and form while angels are forms without matter; created things and God both have being, but in created things essence and existence are distinct and in God they are not; and so forth. The being of an accident is *analogous* to that of a substance, that of a material thing is *analogous* to that of an angel, and that of a created thing is *analogous* to that of God; that is to say, it is neither completely identical nor absolutely incomparable.

Being is also what is called in Thomistic philosophy a *transcendental*, something above every genus, common to all beings and thus not restricted to any category or individual. The other transcendentals, on Aquinas's account, are *thing*, *one*, *something*, *true*, and *good*, and each is "convertible" with being in the sense that each designates one and the same thing – namely being – under a different aspect (*QDV* 1.1). (To put the point in terms made familiar by the logician Gottlob Frege, the transcendentals differ in *sense* but not in *reference*, referring to the same thing under different names just as "Superman" and "Clark Kent" do.) This may be clearest in the cases of *thing* and *something*, since a "thing" is just a being of some kind or other, and "something" connotes either a being among other beings, or being as opposed to non-being or nothing. *One* (to oversimplify a bit) is meant in more or less the former of these senses of "something," as connoting one being distinct from others. The idea of convertibility is, for modern readers anyway, hardest to understand in the cases of *true* and *good*, since truth is usually understood by contemporary philosophers as an attribute confined to beliefs and propositions, and goodness is regarded by many to be a matter of "value" rather than "fact."

With respect to truth, it is useful, in understanding what Aquinas is saying, to think of "true" in the sense of "real" or "genuine." A thing is true to the extent that it conforms to the ideal defined by the essence of the kind it belongs to. Hence a triangle drawn sloppily on the cracked plastic seat of a moving school bus is not as true a triangle as one drawn slowly and carefully on paper with a Rapidograph pen and a ruler, for since its sides will be less straight it will less perfectly instantiate the essence of triangularity; a squirrel which due to injury or genetic defect has lost its tail or its desire to gather nuts for the winter is not as true a squirrel as one who still has its tail, its normal desires, and whatever other features flow from the essence of squirrels; and so forth. Now as we have seen, for Aquinas such essences, when considered as universals, exist only in the intellect; and following St. Augustine, Aquinas regards these universals as existing first and foremost in the divine intellect, as the archetypes according to which God creates the world (*ST* I.15.1). Thus, in a sense, "the word 'true' ... expresses the conformity of a being to intellect" (*QDV* 1.1), whether a human intellect which grasps a universal, or (ultimately) the divine intellect in which the universal exists eternally. Hence something *has being* as the kind of thing it is precisely to the extent that it is *a true instance* of that kind, as defined by the universal essence existing in the intellect; and in that sense being is convertible with truth.

This also gives a clue as to how *good* is convertible with being. Philosophers in the classical (as opposed to modern) tradition, such as Plato, Aristotle, Augustine, and Aquinas, tend to think of goodness in terms of conformity to the ideal represented by a thing's nature or essence. To take the triangle example again, it is natural to describe the well-drawn triangle as not merely a *true* triangle, but also as a *good* triangle, and the poorly drawn triangle as a *bad* one. "Good" or "bad" are to be understood here in the sense in which we describe something as a good or bad specimen or example of a type of thing; and as this makes evident, the terms are therefore being used in a sense that is broader than (though as we shall see, it also encompasses) the moral sense of "good" and "bad." As with *true*, then, something is *good* to the extent that it exists as, or has being as, an instance of its kind. As Aquinas says, "everything is perfect so far as it is actual. Therefore it is clear that a thing is perfect so far as it exists; for it is existence that makes all things actual" (*ST* I.5.1). Now it is also true that "the essence of goodness consists in this, that it is in some way desirable"; but "a thing is desirable only in so far as it is perfect," and thus to the extent that it is actual or exists (*ST* I.5.1). "Hence it is clear that goodness and being are the same really. But goodness presents the aspect of desirableness, which being does not present" (*ST* I.5.1).

This last part of the argument is liable to be badly misunderstood if it is not kept in mind that by "desirable" Aquinas does *not* mean that which conforms to some desire we happen contingently to have, nor even, necessarily, anything desired in a conscious way. Here as elsewhere, it is the notion of the final cause – the end or goal towards which a thing is directed *by nature* – that is key (*ST* I.5.4). As we have seen, a thing's final cause, and thus that which it "desires" (in the relevant sense), might be something of which it is totally unconscious, as in the case of inanimate natural objects and processes; in creatures with intellects, such as ourselves, it might even be something we consciously (if irrationally) try to avoid realizing. But since the realization of a thing's good is what it is *by its nature* directed towards as its final cause, we see that Aquinas's dictum (borrowed from Aristotle) that "goodness is that which all things desire" (*ST* I.5.4) is, when properly understood, not a dubious piece of armchair psychology, but rather (given his basic ontological commitments) a necessary truth of metaphysics.

The claim that being is convertible with goodness might nevertheless seem to be falsified by the existence of evil. For if evil exists, then (so it might be thought) it must have being; and since evil is the opposite of good, it would seem to follow that there is something having being that is nevertheless not good. But Aquinas would deny the first premise of this argument. He writes that "it cannot be that evil signifies being, or any form or nature. Therefore it must be that by the name of evil is signified the absence of good. And this is what is meant by saying that *evil is neither a being nor a good*. For since being, as such, is good, the absence of one implies the absence of the other" (*ST* I.48.1). Precisely because good is convertible with being, evil, which is the opposite of good, cannot itself be a kind of being but rather the absence of being. In particular, it is what the Scholastic philosophers called a *privation*, the absence of some perfection which should be present in a thing given its nature. Hence blindness (for example) is not a kind of being or positive reality, but rather simply the absence of sight in some creature which by its nature should have it. Its existence, and that of other evils, thus does not conflict with the claim that *being* is convertible with *good*.

Final causality

To many modern readers, several aspects of Aquinas's metaphysics might seem quaint, of historical interest perhaps but irrelevant to contemporary philosophical debates. In particular, the principle of finality, on which (as we have seen) virtually the whole of his metaphysics depends, might be thought to have been decisively refuted by modern science, which more or less officially banished the appeal to final causes from scientific method several centuries ago. It must be said, however, that those who make this assumption – and it is a very common assumption indeed – generally do not seem to understand either the notion of final causality, nor the nature of the intellectual revolution represented by the rise of modern science, nor the extent to which appeals to final causality, in substance if not by name, still permeate contemporary mainstream philosophy and science. There is in fact a strong case to be made that final causality is unavoidable if we are to make sense, not only of human thought and action, but also of what we know about the natural world in general from modern physical science itself.

I have already noted how some common assumptions about final causality – such as the idea that it involves attributing quasi-biological functions or conscious awareness to everything, including inanimate objects – are simply false. To the extent that contemporary philosophers find the principle of finality implausible, then, their misgivings are at least in part based on misunderstandings. Also problematic are the arguments early modern thinkers tended to give to justify their rejection of appeals to final causality. Descartes claimed that the appeal to final causes arrogantly but falsely assumes that we can know the intentions of God, the author of the final causes of things. But there are two problems with this. First, even if we could not know the final causes of things, it would not follow (as Descartes himself seems to have granted) that final causality does not exist; and the mere existence of final causality would suffice to justify many of the metaphysical conclusions Aquinas and other Scholastic thinkers based upon it. For example, even if we could not know specifically *what* the final cause of this or that natural phenomenon is, as long as it actually *had* one we would have the basis for an argument for God's existence of the sort represented by Aquinas's Fifth Way, as we shall see in the next chapter. Second, even if there are many phenomena whose final causes we do not and perhaps cannot know – and Aquinas and the other Scholastics never denied this – it seems obvious that there are also many phenomena whose final causes we *can* know. For example, if the eye has a final cause at all, it is surely obvious that it has to do with seeing; if the heart has a final cause at all, it is obvious that it has to do with pumping blood; and so forth.

Perhaps the most famous criticism of Scholastic metaphysics on the part of the early modern thinkers is the one represented by Molière's joke about the doctor who claimed to explain why opium causes sleep by saying that it has a "dormitive power." The reason this is supposed to be funny is that "dormitive power" means "a power to cause sleep," so that the doctor's explanation amounts to saying "Opium causes sleep because it has a power to cause sleep." The reason this is supposed to be a criticism of the metaphysics defended by Aquinas and other Scholastics – which, as we have seen, held that efficient causes are directed towards certain effects as their final causes, so that they can be said to have inherent "powers" to bring about those effects – is that it shows (so it is said) that the explanations provided by Scholastic metaphysics are vacuous tautologies. But though the explanation in question in this case is not very informative, it is not in fact a tautology; it does have substantial content, however minimal. To say "Opium causes sleep because it causes sleep" *would* be a tautology, but the statement in question says more than that. It says that opium has a *power* to cause sleep; that is to say, it tells us that the fact that sleep tends to follow the taking of opium is not an accidental feature of this or that sample of opium, but belongs to the nature of opium as such. That this is not a tautology is evidenced by the fact that early modern thinkers tended to regard it as false, rather than (as they should have done were it really a tautology) trivially true. They didn't say: "Yes, opium has the power to cause sleep, but that's too obvious to be worth mentioning"; they said: "No, opium has no such power, because 'powers,' 'final causes,' and the like don't exist." So, the critique of Scholasticism implied in Molière's joke is muddled. Moreover, while it is true to say that the appeal to opium's inherent powers doesn't give us the sort of satisfying detailed empirical account of opium's nature that modern chemistry would, it is important to understand that it is not intended to do so. Its point is rather to state a basic metaphysical truth that underlies the empirical details about opium's chemical structure, whatever they turn out to be.

It is also sometimes thought that the findings of modern science, which have refuted various assumptions of Aristotelian science, thereby refute Aristotelian metaphysics. But that is a non sequitur. Aristotelian physics is one thing, and Aristotelian metaphysics another, and they do not stand or fall together. Even if some of the scientific examples in terms of which Aristotelians sometimes explained their metaphysical notions have turned out to be false – such as the idea that the earth sits motionless at the center of the universe – there is no essential connection between the metaphysical notions and the scientific examples, and the former can easily be restated in terms of better examples. Nor was the possibility of empirical scientific advance denied by the Scholastic thinkers, as if they thought the science of their time infallible. As Aquinas himself says with respect to the Ptolemaic astronomy accepted in his day, "the suppositions that these astronomers have invented need not necessarily be true; for perhaps the phenomena of the stars are explicable on some other plan not yet discovered by men" (*In DC* II.17, as translated by Rickaby at p. 67 of his *Scholasticism*; cf. *ST* I.32.1).

Of course, the founders of modern science – Galileo, Descartes, Boyle, Newton, et al. – did indeed differ from the Aristotelians over metaphysics too, and not just on empirical details. In particular, they differed over what metaphysical assumptions ought to guide empirical scientific inquiry, holding that final causes and the like ought to be eschewed in favor of "mechanical" (i.e. non-teleological) explanations, and that a mathematical description of nature was preferable to the Aristotelians' appeal to such unquantifiable notions as inherent powers and substantial forms. And of course, this new conception of scientific method has had tremendous success. It is fallacious, however, to infer (as is often done) from the success of the modern mechanistic-cum-quantificational scientific method to the falsity of the Aristotelian scheme it replaced, for the "success" in question has nothing necessarily to do with an attempt to get at the deep ontological structure of reality (a project about which modern thinkers have if anything tended to be rather skeptical). In fact, the moderns' preference for the new method seems to have been motivated less by any purported metaphysical superiority it had over Aristotelianism – again, the philosophical arguments made in its favor were in general surprisingly feeble – than by a practical interest in reorienting philosophy and science to improving the material conditions of human life in this world. The ancients and the medievals had tended to regard intellectual inquiry as a search for wisdom, understood as knowledge of the ultimate causes and meaning of things, in light of which one might improve one's soul and prepare for a life beyond this one. By contrast, the early modern thinkers tended to see it rather as a means of increasing "human utility and power" through the "mechanical arts" or technology (in the words of Francis Bacon) and of making us "masters and possessors of nature" (as Descartes put it). Such technological advancement would be facilitated by a quantificational approach to the study of nature; hence the attractiveness of this approach to the moderns. The early modern thinkers were also wary of the tendency of Aristotelian Scholasticism to shore up the exist-ing political and religious order, as it was bound to do given its talk of the fixed essences and final causes of things, including human beings and human societies. This order was, after all, highly conservative and decidedly "otherworldly" in its orienta-tion, and thus out of sync with the project of improving life in the here and now. Any replacement of the Aristotelian scheme, such as the new mechanistic-cum-mathematical conception of nature afforded, thus had definite political as well as practical advantages.

If the new science of the moderns has "succeeded," then, it might be argued that this is in large part because they stacked the deck in their own favor. Having redefined "success" as the achievement of dramatic technological progress and in general the manipulation of nature to achieve human ends, they essen-tially won a game the Scholastics were not trying to play in the first place. That is not to say that the Aristotelians entirely eschewed the quantificational approach to science or the technological advances it makes possible; in fact some late Scholastic thinkers did put greater emphasis on quantificational methods, and Galileo and other early modern scientists built on their work. But their emphasis was on formal and final causes and the like, because they took these to be more fundamental to our understanding of the nature of things and to yield knowledge that had greater moral and theological significance. And they would also have emphasized that to focus obsessively on one aspect of reality, though this will undoubtedly increase one's knowledge of that aspect, does nothing to show that there are no other aspects worth studying – aspects that might be even more important, and apart from which our understanding of the first aspect might become distorted. In particular, if you insist on looking only for those features of nature that can be described in the language of mathematics, then of course that is all you are going to find; and if you refuse to look for or even to acknowledge the existence of final causes, then it is hardly surprising if you do not discover any. Obviously, though, it doesn't follow that there are no final causes or non-quantifiable aspects of nature, any more than a refusal to remove one's red spectacles would "prove" that everything is red. To pretend that this does follow is simply to let one's method dictate what counts as reality, rather than letting reality determine one's method.

The mechanistic denial of final causes, inherent powers, and the like did not follow from the science, then, but was read into the science from the beginning. What is often regarded as a "discovery" arrived at via empirical scientific inquiry was in fact a stipulation concerning the nature of scientific method, a limitation, more or less by fiat, of what would be allowed to *count* as "scientific." As historian and philosopher of science E. A. Burtt concluded in his classic *The Metaphysical Foundations of Modern Physical Science*, the founders of the mechanistic-cum-mathematical conception of nature were driven by "wishful thinking" and "uncritical confidence" of just the sort of which they accused the Aristotelian Scholastic tradition they sought to overthrow; final causes and the like were regarded by them as "sources of distraction [which] simply had to be denied or removed" (pp. 305–6).

If there is much less to the moderns' case against Aristotelianism than meets the eye, it might yet be suggested that the point is moot, insofar as the modern mechanistic, quantificational picture of the natural world has proven itself capable of accounting for all of reality in any event. There is, on this view, simply no *need* to appeal to final causes, substantial forms, inherent powers and the like. But any such suggestion would be – not to put too fine a point on it – question-begging, naïve, and historically ill informed. The fact is that a myriad of philosophical problems – indeed, many problems that have misleadingly come to be regarded as "perennial" or "traditional" problems of philosophy – arose only after and because of the early modern philosophers' abandonment of key Aristotelian and Scholastic notions. As Alasdair MacIntyre has argued, the plethora of competing moral theories within modern philosophy – not to mention the radical disagreement that has come to exist within Western society at large over the grounds and content of morality, and widespread skepticism about whether this disagreement is susceptible of any rational, objective adjudication – is a consequence of the abandonment of a teleological conception of human life in particular and the natural world in general. (We will have reason to return to this theme in chapter 5.) As we shall see in chapter 4, the "mind–body problem" as it has been understood since the time of Descartes and the "problem of personal identity" as it has been debated since the time of Locke are largely byproducts of the early modern philosophers' abandonment of the notion of formal causation. Even the problems of free will and skepticism, though they have been discussed in one form or another for millennia, owe (as I have argued at length elsewhere) their modern, seemingly intractable character to the abandonment of certain key Aristotelian metaphysical assumptions. If the exclusively mechanistic and quantitative conception of nature that the moderns replaced Scholasticism with has led to such philosophical puzzlement, it is hardly plausible to suggest that there are no grounds for a reconsideration of their decision.

This should perhaps be most evident from what modern philosophers have made of causation, that metaphysical notion which is most fundamental to the natural science modern philosophy claims to champion. As we have seen, for Aristotle and Aquinas, we cannot make sense of efficient causation – which is, of Aristotle's four causes, the one modern philosophers find most familiar – apart from final causation. As we have also seen (and as is well known in any case) efficient causation has indeed become something modern philosophers have found it very difficult to make sense of in light of the puzzles raised by Hume – puzzles that seem to arise only if we deny that causes are inherently "directed towards" their effects as towards a final cause. In particular, it has been notoriously difficult for modern philosophy to account for the necessary connection that common sense supposes to hold between causes and effects. This difficulty has in turn led to the "problem of induction," on which, since there is no necessary connection between causes and effects, there seems also to be no rational ground for inferences to the unobserved from the observed or to the future based on what has happened in the past. Yet if science is in the business of discovering objective causal relationships between things, of describing the world in general (the unobserved portions as well as the observed ones), and of making predictions on the basis of that description, then it seems that science is impossible, or at least rationally unfounded. The "mechanistic" or non-teleological picture of the natural world that purportedly made modern natural science possible in fact seems to make it unintelligible.

The conceptual incoherence within ethics which MacIntyre has argued followed upon the moderns' abandonment of teleology thus has, arguably, a parallel within modern metaphysics. Efficient causality becomes unintelligible without final causality; substance, and particularly that substance we call the human person, becomes unintelligible without the hylemorphic distinction between form and matter; free will becomes unintelligible when we insist on reducing human action to bodily movements governed by chains of efficient causation, and ignore those descriptions in terms of formal and final causation apart from which it cannot be understood as *action* in the first place; and so on. These are, of course, large issues; again, I have addressed them at greater length elsewhere (in works cited in the Further Reading section), and we will return to several of them in the course of this book. Suffice it for now to note that there is much about modern philosophy to indicate that the recent revival of interest in Aristotle's moral theory ought to be met by a serious reconsideration of Aristotelian metaphysics as well.

There is much in modern science to indicate the same thing. Consider first the findings of modern biology. Darwinian evolutionary theory was, officially at least, supposed at long last to exorcise final causality from that part of the natural world where its existence seems most obvious. And yet, as the Thomist philosopher Etienne Gilson documented at length in his *From Aristotle to Darwin and Back Again*, teleological concepts have permeated Darwinian theory from the beginning. One problem here is that even after Darwin, it is as impossible as it ever was to give an adequate description of an animal's organs, behavioral patterns, and the like except in terms of what they are *for*, and thus in teleological language. Contemporary philosophers of biology have tried to show how such language can be "cashed out" or analyzed in non-teleological terms, but no such proposal has been without serious problems. For example, on the currently most popular theory, to say that the kidneys in such-and-such an organism serve the function of purifying the blood is just shorthand for saying something like this: those ancestors of this organism who first developed kidneys (as a result of a random genetic mutation) tended to survive in greater numbers than those without kidneys, because their blood happened thereby to get purified; and this caused the gene for kidneys to get passed on to the organism in question and others like it. But as John Searle has pointed out, strictly speaking, such Darwinian accounts of the origins of biological traits don't provide an "analysis" or "explanation" of the teleological functions of those traits at all, but rather simply *eliminate* the notion of teleology altogether, treating it as at best a kind of useful fiction. To use Aristotelian terminology, they are attempts to discard final causality and explain biological phenomena entirely in terms of efficient causality, not attempts to reduce final causality to efficient causality (a project which seems incoherent in any event). Moreover, even if we took such accounts seriously as analyses of teleological function, they would face serious difficulties. As Jerry Fodor has noted, they seem to have the absurd implications that we cannot know the function of a thing unless we know how it evolved, and that nothing could in principle even *have* a biological function unless it evolved. But in fact we knew the functions of all sorts of organs and behaviors long before the idea of natural selection ever occurred to anyone, and it is at least theoretically possible that such organs and behaviors could have functions even if they did not evolve.

A deeper problem, though, is that what may be the greatest discovery of modern biology – DNA and the genetic code it embodies (which have been incorporated into the Darwinian story about the evolution of life) – seems teleological through and through. Descriptions of this famous molecule make constant reference to the "information," "data," "instructions," "blueprint," "software," "programming," and so on contained within it; and for good reason, since there is simply no way accurately to convey what DNA does without the use of such concepts. But every single one of them entails that DNA is "directed towards" something beyond itself as a kind of "end" or "goal" – the development of this organ in the growing organism, the manifestation of such and such a behavioral tendency, or what have you – and thus manifests precisely the sort of final causality that modern biology is claimed to have swept away.

It is important to note that this has nothing whatsoever to do with the "irreducible complexity" that "Intelligent Design" theorists claim certain biological phenomena exhibit; the Aristotelian need not take sides in the debate between Darwinian biologists and "Intelligent Design" theorists (who generally accept the mechanistic view of nature endorsed by their materialist opponents). Final causality is evident in DNA not because of how complex it is, but because of what it does, and would be equally evident however simple in physical structure DNA might have been. As the physicist Paul Davies notes in his book *The Fifth Miracle*, "concepts like information and software … [involve] notions that are quite alien to the physicist's description of the world" – a description which is (again, at least officially) supposed to be entirely mechanistic – and the use of such concepts in biology "treat[s] semantic information as if it were a natural quantity like energy." "Unfortunately," continues Davies,

> "meaning" sounds perilously close to purpose, an utterly taboo subject in biology. So we are left with the contradiction that we need to apply concepts derived from purposeful human activities (communication, meaning, context, semantics) to biological processes that certainly appear purposeful, but are in fact not (or are not supposed to be).

Concludes Davies,

> at the end of the day, human beings are products of nature, and if humans have purposes, then at some level purposefulness

must arise from nature and therefore be inherent in nature …
Might purpose be a genuine property of nature right down to
the cellular or even the subcellular level? (p. 121–2)

Davies seems close to a position expressed decades earlier by the
biophysicist and Nobel laureate Max Delbrück, who once wrote
that if the Nobel Prize could be awarded posthumously, "I think
they should consider Aristotle for the discovery of the principle
implied in DNA," and that "the reason for the lack of appreci-
ation, among scientists, of Aristotle's scheme lies in our having
been blinded for 300 years by the Newtonian view of the
world."

Part of the reason the Aristotelian regards efficient causality
as unintelligible without final causality is that without the notion
of an end or goal towards which an efficient cause naturally
points, there is no way to make sense of why certain causal
chains are significant in a way others are not. For example, in
characterizing the DNA of bears, we take it to be relevant to
note that it causes them to be furry and to grow to a large size,
but not that it also thereby causes them to be good mascots for
football teams. The genetic information in bear DNA inherently
"points to" or is "directed at" the first outcome, but not the
second. But this sort of consideration applies to causal chains
generally, including inorganic ones. As the philosopher David
Oderberg has noted, it is particularly evident in natural cycles
like the water cycle and the rock cycle. In the former case,
condensation leads to precipitation, which leads to collection,
which leads to evaporation, which leads to condensation, and
the cycle begins again. In the latter case, igneous rock forms into
sedimentary rock, which forms into metamorphic rock, which
melts into magma, which hardens into igneous rock, and the
cycle begins again. Scientists who study these processes identify
each of their stages as playing a certain specific role relative to
the others. For example, the role of condensation in the water

cycle is to bring about precipitation; the role of pressure in the rock cycle is, in conjunction with heat, to contribute to generating magma, and in the absence of heat to contribute to generating sedimentary rock; and so forth. Each stage has the production of some particular outcome or range of outcomes as an "end" or "goal" towards which it points. Nor will it do to suggest that either cycle could be adequately described by speaking of each stage as being the efficient cause of certain others, with no reference to its playing a "role" of generating some effect as an "end" or "goal." For each stage has many other effects that are not part of the cycle. As Oderberg points out, sedimentation might (for example) happen to block the water flow to a certain region, the formation of magma might cause some local birds to migrate, or condensation in some area might for all we know cause someone to have arthritic pain in his big toe. But blocking water flow and causing birds to migrate are no part of the rock cycle, and causing arthritic pain is no part of the water cycle. Some causal chains are relevant to the cycles and some are not. Nor is it correct to say that the student of the rock or water cycles just happens to be interested in the way some rock generates other kinds and how water in one form brings about water in another form, and is not interested in bird migration patterns or arthritis, so that he pays attention to some elements in the overall causal situation rather than others. For the patterns described by scientists studying these cycles are *objective* patterns in nature, not mere projections of human interests. But the only way to account for this is to recognize that each stage in the process, while it might have various sorts of effects, has only the generation of certain *specific* effects among them as its "end" or "goal" and that this is what determines its role in the cycle. In short, it is to recognize such cycles as teleological.

Finally, let us consider basic causal laws of the sort studied by physicists. The founders of modern philosophy, keen to eliminate substantial forms, natures, essences, powers, final causes, and the like from science, sought to replace them with the idea of events related by "laws of nature." Hence, when a brick is thrown at a window and the window shatters, it's not (on this view) that the brick, by virtue of its nature or essence, has an inherent power to break glass, or that it is inherently directed towards this sort of outcome as a final cause. It is rather that events like the throwing of bricks just happen to be regularly followed, in a lawlike way, by events like the shattering of windows.

As philosopher of science Nancy Cartwright has argued, a serious problem with the idea that science is merely in the business of establishing regularities on the basis of observation is that the sorts of regularities that the hard sciences tend to uncover are rarely observed, and in fact are in ordinary circumstances impossible to observe. Beginning students of physics quickly become acquainted with idealizations like the notion of a frictionless surface, and with the fact that laws like Newton's law of gravitation strictly speaking describe the behavior of bodies only in the circumstance where no interfering forces are acting on them, a circumstance which never actually holds. Moreover, physicists do not in fact embrace a regularity as a law of nature only after many trials, after the fashion of popular presentations of inductive reasoning. Rather, they draw their conclusions from a few highly specialized experiments conducted under artificial conditions. None of this is consistent with the idea that science is concerned with cataloguing observed regularities. But it is consistent with the Aristotelian picture of science as in the business of uncovering the hidden natures or powers of things. Actual experimental practice indicates that what physicists are really looking for are the inherent powers a thing will naturally manifest when interfering conditions are removed, and the fact that a few experiments, or even a single controlled experiment, are taken to establish the results in question indicates that these powers are taken to reflect a nature that is universal to things of that type.

Cartwright's views are by no means idiosyncratic. They reflect a growing trend within the philosophy of science towards a neo-Aristotelian "new essentialism," as Brian Ellis, one of its proponents, has labeled it. Nor is it just Aristotle's doctrine of natures, forms, or essences that finds an echo in the new essentialism. As many of these theorists have recognized, to affirm the existence in physical phenomena of inherent powers or capacities is to acknowledge phenomena that are directed at or point to states of affairs beyond themselves. For example, to be fragile is to point to or be directed at *breaking*, and a fragile thing of its nature points to or is directed at this particular state even if it is never in fact realized; to be soluble is to point to or be directed at *dissolving*, and a soluble thing of its nature points to or is directed at this particular state even if it is never in fact realized; and so forth. The late "new essentialist" philosopher George Molnar concluded that the powers inherent in physical objects exhibit a kind of "physical intentionality" insofar as, like thoughts and other mental states, they point to something beyond themselves, even though they are unlike thoughts in being unconscious. But the notion of something which points beyond itself to a certain goal or end-state even though it is totally unconscious is, of course, nothing other than the Aristotelian notion of final causality. As Cartwright has said, "the empiricists of the scientific revolution wanted to oust Aristotle entirely from the new learning," but "they did no such thing."

The reference to intentionality – the mind's capacity to represent, refer, or point beyond itself – should bring to mind the most obvious examples of natural phenomena difficult to account for in mechanistic terms, namely human thought and action. When you think about the Eiffel Tower, say, your thought is "directed towards" something beyond itself in a way analogous to the manner in which a match is, on the Aristotelian analysis, "directed towards" the generation of flame and heat as its final cause. Similarly, when you reason through an argument, your thought process is "directed towards" the conclusion as the end towards which the premises point. But precisely because the physical world is, on a mechanistic account, devoid of any end- or goal-directedness, the existence of our thoughts and thought processes would seem impossible to explain in purely physical terms. (Indeed, this is no doubt part of the reason Descartes was a dualist: given his mechanistic conception of the material world, there was nowhere else for human thought to exist except in something immaterial.) Similarly, human actions seem just obviously teleological in nature, directed towards certain ends for the sake of which they are carried out; at least, and as philosophers like G. F. Schueler and Scott Sehon have argued at length, no attempt to analyze human action in non-teleological terms has succeeded.

From human thought and action to the world of biological phenomena in general to inorganic natural cycles to the basic laws of physics, final causality or teleology thus seems as real and objective a feature of the natural world as Aristotle and Aquinas took it to be. At the very least, their conception of final causal-ity is surely defensible and worthy of the serious consideration of contemporary philosophers.

Efficient causality

If the principle of finality can be defended, then, what of the other two Aristotelian principles I have said are crucial to Aquinas's metaphysics in general and his arguments for God's existence in particular – namely, the principle of causality and the principle of proportionate causality (which concern efficient rather than final causality)?

To take the latter first, it is worth noting that it is certainly supported by common sense. If you come across a puddle of red liquid near a faucet, you will not suppose that the water in the faucet caused the puddle all by itself. The reason is that water, on its own, does not have within it what is required to generate the effect in question. A leaky faucet by itself might produce a puddle, but not a red one. Hence, you will conclude either that the puddle was caused by something else – a spilled can of soda pop, maybe, or someone bleeding – or that it was caused by the water from the faucet in conjunction with something else, such as a "fizzy" tablet dropped in a water puddle or even heavy rust in the water line. In reasoning in this fashion you would be evincing a tacit commitment to the principle of proportionate causality, viz. that a cause cannot give to its effect what it does not have itself, whether formally, eminently, or virtually.

It is nevertheless sometimes suggested that this principle is disproved by evolution, since if simpler life forms give rise to more complex ones then (it is claimed) they must surely be producing in their effects something they did not have to give. But this does not follow. Every species is essentially just a variation on the same basic genetic material that has existed for billions of years from the moment life began. On the Darwinian story, a new variation arises when there is a mutation in the existing genetic structure which produces a trait that happens to be advantageous given circumstances in a creature's environment. The mutation in turn might be caused by a copying error made during the DNA replication process or by some external factor like radiation or chemical damage. Just as water in conjunction with something else might be sufficient to produce a red puddle even if the water by itself wouldn't be, so too do the existing genetic material, the mutation, and environmental circumstances together generate a new biological variation even though none of these factors by itself would be sufficient to do so. Thus, evolution no more poses a challenge to the principle of proportionate causality than the puddle example does. Indeed, as Paul Davies points out in *The Fifth Miracle* (cited earlier), to deny that the information contained in a new kind of life form derives from some combination of preexisting factors – specifically, in part from the organism's environment if not from its genetic inheritance alone – would contradict the second law of thermodynamics, which tells us that order (and thus information content) tends inevitably to decrease, not increase, within a closed system.

The principle of causality was famously challenged by Hume, who claimed, as we noted earlier, that we can easily conceive of a thing coming into being without any cause at all. What he has in mind is something like imagining the surface of a table which at first has nothing on it, but on which a bowling ball suddenly appears, "out of nowhere" as it were. But there are several problems with the suggestion that this exercise in imagination entails conceiving of something coming into being uncaused. First, it falsely assumes that to imagine something – that is, to form a mental image of it – is the same as to conceive it, in the sense of forming a coherent intellectual idea of it. But imagining something and conceiving it in the intellect are not the same thing. You can form no clear mental image of a chiliagon – a 1,000-sided figure – certainly not one that's at all distinct from your mental image of a 997-sided figure or a 1,002-sided figure. Still, your intellect can easily grasp the concept of a chiliagon. You can form no mental image of a triangle that is not equilateral, isosceles, or scalene. But the concept of triangularity that exists in your intellect, which abstracts away from these features of concrete triangles, applies equally to all of them. And so forth. Like many empiricists, Hume conflates the intellect and the imagination, and his argument sounds plausible only if one follows him in committing this error.

Second, as Elizabeth Anscombe pointed out, to imagine something appearing suddenly isn't even to *imagine* it (let alone conceive it) coming into existence without a cause. Suppose the situation described really happened to you: a bowling ball suddenly appears on your table. Your spontaneous reaction would surely *not* be to conclude that it came into existence without a cause; rather, you'd ask "Where did that come from?" ... a question which presupposes that there is a source, a *cause*, from which the bowling ball sprang. You would also no doubt consider all sorts of bizarre explanations – a magician's trick, a mad scientist testing a teleportation device, an astronomically improbable quantum fluctuation in the table – before it would even occur to you that there might be no cause. Indeed, this may never occur to you; should even the most bizarre explanation be ruled out, you would probably think "I guess I'll never know what caused it" – *what* caused it, not whether it was caused. In any event, there's nothing about the kind of situation Hume describes that amounts to imagining something coming into existence with *no* cause, as opposed to coming into existence with an *unknown* or *unusual* cause.

But Hume's argument is more problematic still. Anscombe asks us to consider how we'd go about determining whether the sort of scenario we've been describing really is a case of something *coming into existence* in the first place, as opposed, say, to merely reappearing from somewhere else where it had already existed. And the answer is that the only way we could do so is by making reference to some *cause* of the thing's suddenly being here as being a *creating* cause, specifically, rather than a *transporting* one. So, the only way we can ultimately make sense of something coming into being is by reference to a cause. Thus, what Hume says we can easily conceive not only hasn't been conceived by him, it seems likely impossible to conceive.

It is also sometimes suggested that quantum mechanics undermines the principle of causality insofar as it implies that the world is not deterministic. But the Aristotelian does not regard the world as deterministic in any case (determinism being a view associated with the mechanical conception of nature Aristotelians reject), and thus does not hold that every cause must be a deterministic cause. As the analytical Thomist John

Haldane has noted, if we can appeal to objective, non-deterministic natural propensities in quantum systems to account for the phenomena they exhibit, this will suffice to provide us with the sort of explanation the Aristotelian claims every contingent thing in the world must have.

So the principle of causality seems secure. And it is worth emphasizing that it is a principle that is in any event presupposed in empirical scientific inquiry – which is in the business of searching for the causes of things – and thus in the very activity held up as the paradigm of rationality by those most inclined to challenge the principle of causality, namely atheists seeking to block "First Cause" arguments for God's existence of the sort we'll be examining in the next chapter.

Being

Within recent analytic philosophy, the aspect of Aquinas's thought that has perhaps gotten the most negative attention is his distinction between essence and existence. In particular, Anthony Kenny has alleged that on this subject Aquinas was "thoroughly confused," and that his doctrine of being amounts to little more than "sophistry and illusion."

To understand Kenny's criticisms, it is necessary first briefly to summarize a notion of existence introduced into modern logic by Gottlob Frege (1848–1925). Take a sentence like "Cats exist." At first glance this seems to predicate existence of a certain kind of object, namely cats. But Frege argued that this appearance is misleading. Existence, he claimed, is not a predicate of objects (that is to say, a first-level predicate), but rather a predicate of concepts (that is to say, a second-level predicate). In this case, it is being predicated of the concept *being a cat*. Hence, to reveal the logical structure of the sentence in question, we'd have to rewrite it as saying something like "There is at least one x such that x is a cat." This does not tell us that a certain object has a property or attribute of existence; rather it tells us that there is at least one thing falling under a certain concept. Thus the sentence in question does not tell us something about individual cats, but rather something about the concept of being a cat.

A standard argument for the view that this Fregean notion of existence is the only legitimate notion is that if existence were a first-level predicate of objects, then (it is claimed) negative existential statements like "Martians do not exist" would be self-contradictory, which they obviously are not. For if we think of this statement as saying that Martians do not have the property or attribute of existence, this would seem to entail that there are (i.e. there exist) certain creatures, namely Martians, who lack existence. Since that is absurd, the statement "Martians do not exist" cannot be interpreted as denying a property or attribute of existence to some object or objects. It should rather be interpreted in light of Frege's doctrine of existence as saying something like "It is not the case that there is at least one x such that x is a Martian." That is to say, it says of the concept *being a Martian* that there is nothing to which it applies.

Kenny's central objection to Aquinas (which he borrows from Peter Geach, and develops at length in his book *Aquinas on Being*) is that the doctrine that God's essence is identical to his existence can be seen to be incoherent when read in light of Frege's doctrine of existence. It amounts, he claims, to thinking that the correct answer to the question "What is God?" is "There is one," which would, of course, be an absurd reply. But since "What is God?" is a question about God's essence, and "There is an x such that x is God" is (he holds) what is meant by talking about God's existence, this absurd reply is, Kenny maintains, what Aquinas is in effect putting forward when he claims that God's essence is identical to his existence.

Defenders of Aquinas have replied to Kenny in various ways. Brian Davies, for example, while more or less conceding

Kenny's Fregean analysis of existence, argues that Kenny has misconstrued Aquinas's claim that God's essence and existence are identical. This claim is not (so Davies suggests) an attempt to tell us what God is, but rather a statement about what God is not. It is a piece of "negative theology," rather than a positive characterization of God's nature. In particular, it is telling us that whatever God is, he is not the sort of thing that can intelligibly be said to be capable of non-existence, the way material objects and other contingent things can be. And there is nothing in this that entails the absurd answer to the question "What is God?" that Kenny puts into Aquinas's mouth.

But other Thomists would object that such a reply needlessly waters down Aquinas's doctrine of being and concedes too much to Kenny's criticism. For one thing, it is tendentious to assume that Aquinas is or ought to be operating with a Fregean notion of existence. As Gyula Klima has said, "it is ludicrous to claim victory by yelling 'Checkmate!' in a game of poker. But this is precisely what Kenny seems to be doing whenever he is yelling 'You are not a good enough Fregean!' at Aquinas." Certainly other conceptions of existence are possible. Indeed, Kenny himself (again following Geach) distinguishes between "specific existence," which is the Fregean sort captured in statements of the form "There is an x such that …" and "individual existence," which he concedes *is* genuinely predicated of an object, as it is in (to borrow Kenny's example) a sentence like "The Great Pyramid still exists, but the Library of Alexandria does not." "Individual existence," that is to say, is just that which the Library of Alexandria lost when it was destroyed, but which the Great Pyramid still has. Now Kenny allows that the doctrine that God's essence and existence are identical might be interpreted as saying that God has "individual existence" in an everlasting way. But he does not think that even this notion of existence can save Aquinas's position, at least not if that position is to remain interesting. For, he argues, the most that it could sensibly mean to say that God's essence is identical to his "individual existence" in this sense is that as long as God is God he has "individual existence." And this, Kenny says, is true of everything; for example, as long as some dog Fido is Fido he will have "individual existence" too. So "individual existence," Kenny concludes, is useless in spelling out a notion of existence on which God's essence is identical to his existence while in everything else essence and existence are distinct. Yet as Klima complains, this argument of Kenny's (like his earlier one) simply refuses even to try to understand Aquinas's notion of existence in logical terms Aquinas himself would have accepted, instead of in post-Fregean terms. In particular, it fails to consider the possibility of reading "exists" as having *analogous* rather than univocal senses (a distinction explained above in the section on the transcendentals) in "Fido exists" and "God exists," where such a reading would obviously at least open up the possibility that to say that *as long as God is God, he exists*, is to make a *stronger* claim than to say that *as long as Fido is Fido, he exists*. (We might add, with Barry Miller, that since Aquinas's doctrine of divine simplicity holds that God's being *is* his power which *is* his knowledge which *is* his goodness, and so forth, there is clearly more content to Aquinas's conception of God's being than Kenny lets on. We will examine the notion of divine simplicity in the next chapter.)

There is, in any event, ample reason to doubt that the Fregean notion of existence captures everything that needs to be captured by an analysis of existence. Consider that when we are told that "Cats exist" means "There is at least one x such that x is a cat" or that something falls under the concept *being a cat*, there is still the question of *what makes this the case*, of what it is exactly *in virtue of which* there is something falling under this concept. And the answer to this further question is (as David Braine and John Knasas have pointed out) what Aquinas is getting at in his talk of an "act of existing" which is distinct from the essence of a thing (in this case, a cat) but which must be joined to it if the thing is to be real.

In reply to what I referred to above as the standard argument for the exclusive legitimacy of the Fregean analysis of existence, Knasas denies that regarding existence as a first-level predicate has the absurd implication that "Martians do not exist" is self-contradictory. For this would follow only if, when we grasp the concept *Martians*, we necessarily already grasp it as applying to something existing in reality, so that "Martians do not exist" amounts to "The existing Martians do not exist," which of course is self-contradictory. But statements attributing existence or non-existence to a thing, Knasas says, do not function logically in the same way other attributive statements do. In particular, their subjects are grasped in an existence-neutral way. In the case at hand, our mere grasp of the concept *Martians* does not by itself entail either a judgment that they exist or a judgment that they do not, but leaves the question open. "Martians do not exist" thus says, not "The existing Martians do not exist," but rather something like "Martians, which are of themselves existentially neutral, do not in fact exist." In general, for Knasas as for Aquinas, when the mind grasps the essence of a thing it grasps it as something distinct from its act of existing (or lack thereof), even if that of which the act of existing is ultimately predicated is the thing itself and not a mere concept. Of course, modern post-Fregean philosophers might disagree with this, but the mere fact of this disagreement doesn't prove that Aquinas is wrong. Here, as with the issue of final causality, contemporary philosophers need to keep in mind that the fact that Aquinas's basic philosophical assumptions are very different from their own does not by itself have any tendency to show that Aquinas's assumptions are the mistaken ones or that they should not be taken seriously as live options today.

The "essence" as well as the "existence" side of Aquinas's doctrine of being has also come in for criticism from Kenny. In particular, he objects to Aquinas's account of angels as pure forms or essences. He argues that, unlike Plato's humanity, which is predicated of Plato in "Plato is human," "a pure form would be something that corresponded to a predicate in a sentence that had no subject; but this seems close to an absurdity" (p. 30). Likewise, he implies in the same passage that Aquinas's conception of angels is that of "forms inhering in no substances." But this misrepresents Aquinas's position. Aquinas does, after all, refer to angels as "separated *substances*," so it is odd that Kenny should attribute to him the view he does. And what they are separated *from* is not a subject or a substance, but matter. This separation from matter is also what is meant by calling an angel a "pure form." Aquinas does not mean by this expression that an angel is a form *full stop*, as if there were nothing more to be said; as we have seen, he regards an angel as a form or essence *conjoined to an act of existing*. Hence the particular subject or substance that a certain angel (Gabriel, say) is identifiable with should be obvious: it is Gabriel's form conjoined with his individual act of existing. This also gives us the answer to a rhetorical question Kenny raises: "What, we wonder, is the difference between the angelic pure forms that Aquinas accepts and the Platonic Ideas or Forms that he rejects?" (p. 30). The difference is that an angelic pure form is a concrete (though immaterial) particular, with its own individual act of existing, while a Platonic Form is a universal.

Aquinas's realism about essences, then, is consistently moderate or Aristotelian rather than Platonic. We might note that, like his commitment to final causality, this moderate realism is an aspect of his metaphysics that finds significant support in the "new essentialist" philosophy of science described earlier, which regards physical science as in the business of discovering the essences of things (with "essence" given a decidedly Aristotelian accent by these philosophers). But then, essentialism has been making something of a comeback in contemporary philosophy more generally, as evidenced by the work of Kripke and Putnam mentioned above. And even if the Kripke–Putnam form of essentialism must (for the reasons cited earlier) be judged wanting from an Aristotelian point of view, it has at least restored to the philosophical mainstream an awareness of themes that philosophers such as the new essentialists, and, more especially, contemporary analytically oriented Thomists like Klima and Oderberg, have been able to develop in a more sound direction. As the "new essentialist" Crawford Elder has noted, the denial that essences are in some sense objectively real leads to paradox in any case. For if we say that essences are merely the products of human convention, then that would have to include *our* essence, the essence of human beings, as well. But that is incoherent. In order to form conventions in the first place, we have to exist as a species, sharing an essence that constitutes us as such; and if our essence thus makes us what we are, we cannot in turn be that which makes our essence what it is.

All told, Aquinas's doctrine of being and essence, like his understanding of causality in its various forms, is very much alive and something contemporary philosophers have every reason to take seriously – not least because of the roles these doctrines play in Aquinas's arguments in the philosophy of religion, the philosophy of mind, and ethics, as we shall see in the remaining chapters of this book.

3
Natural Theology

Aquinas famously tells us in his *Summa Theologiae* that "the existence of God can be proved in five ways" (*ST* I.2.3). They are (in the order in which he there presents them) the *proof from motion*, the *proof from causality*, the *proof from the contingency of the world*, the *proof from the grades of perfection*, and the *proof from finality*. The short passage in which he states these proofs has appeared in countless anthologies aimed at undergraduates and general readers, and it may be the most famous set of arguments for God's existence ever written. No doubt many readers take the Five Ways to be Aquinas's complete case for the existence of God, indeed, *the* complete case for the existence of God, full stop (apart perhaps from St. Anselm's famous ontological argument). Hence, those who read them and remain unconvinced may conclude from that fact alone that the case for God's existence simply hasn't been made, by Aquinas or likely anyone else.

This is unfortunate, and certainly unfair. To be sure, Aquinas is probably the greatest philosopher of religion in the Western tradition, and though many other thinkers have presented interesting and influential arguments for God's existence, it is not unreasonable to regard Aquinas's work as representative. Moreover, he did think that the best arguments that could be given for God's existence are summarized in the Five Ways. (He rejected Anselm's ontological argument, for reasons we will see later.) But it is crucial to understand that they are *summaries*. Aquinas never intended for them to stand alone, and would probably have reacted with horror if told that future generations of students would be studying them in isolation, removed from their original immediate context in the *Summa Theologiae* and the larger context of his work as a whole. The *Summa*, it must be remembered, was meant as a textbook for beginners in theology who were already Christian believers, not an advanced work in apologetics intended to convince skeptics. The Five Ways themselves are merely short statements of arguments that would already have been well known to the readers of Aquinas's day, and presented at greater length and with greater precision elsewhere. For example, he gives two much more detailed versions of the proof from motion, along with versions of the proofs from causality, the grades of perfection, and finality, in the *Summa contra Gentiles*. The proof from motion, having originated with Aristotle, is also naturally discussed at length in Aquinas's commentaries on Aristotle's *Physics* and *Metaphysics*. The *Commentary on the Sentences*, *On Being and Essence*, *On Truth*, and the *Compendium of Theology* each contain further statements of some of the arguments. Some of them were also familiar from the works of Christian thinkers like St. Augustine, St. John Damascene, and Albert the Great, Muslim thinkers like Avicenna and Averroes, and the Jewish philosopher Moses Maimonides. That the being whose existence Aquinas takes the Five Ways to have proved must have all the divine attributes is something he devotes much of the rest of Part I of the *Summa Theologiae* (as well as hundreds of pages of his other works) to proving. And of course the metaphysical ideas apart from which the Five Ways cannot properly be understood (and which were surveyed in the previous chapter) are developed throughout Aquinas's works.

Torn from this rich context, as they so frequently are, it is no surprise that the Five Ways have been regarded by some readers as anticlimactic or worse. For instance, in his atheistic polemic *The God Delusion*, Richard Dawkins asserts boldly that the arguments "don't prove anything, and are easily – though I hesitate to say so, given [Aquinas's] eminence – exposed as vacuous." But Dawkins' confidence is misplaced, for the objections he makes are based on egregious misunderstandings of the Five Ways of the sort that are bound to arise when one reads only a short anthologized selection from the *Summa* and ignores the metaphysical concepts which underlie the arguments. Dawkins claims, for example, that Aquinas holds that since "there must have been a time when no physical things existed," something must have brought them into being. But in fact Aquinas famously thought that it cannot be proven philosophically that the world had a beginning in time, and while he nevertheless believed it did, he held that this was something that could be known only through divine revelation (*ST* I.46.2). Consequently, his arguments are *not* intended to show that God caused the world to begin at some point in the past (at the Big Bang, say). Rather, he argues that even if the world had always existed, God would still have to exist *here and now*, otherwise certain features that it exhibits *here and now* would be inexplicable. Dawkins also alleges that Aquinas gives "absolutely no reason" to think that the cause of the world must be omnipotent, omniscient, good, and so on. In fact, and as noted already, Aquinas devotes a great many pages to showing this, as anyone who takes the trouble to read the *Summa Theologiae* beyond the passage containing the Five Ways will soon discover. Dawkins thinks that Aquinas's Fifth Way is more or less the same as William Paley's famous "argument from design," when in fact they are radically different, since Aquinas's argument appeals to Aristotelian teleology while Paley's assumes instead a non-teleological mechanistic conception of the natural world. And so forth.

Other common objections to the Five Ways are based on similar misunderstandings. For example, the Second Way is often thought to say that since everything has a cause, the universe too must have a cause, which is what we call God. It is then objected that the argument undermines itself, since if "everything has a cause," then this would have to include God too, in which case he cannot be the first cause. But that is not what the proof says at all. Aquinas does not hold that "*everything has a cause.*" He holds instead only that *that which comes into being*, and more generally *that which is contingent*, must have a cause. (This, you will recall from chapter 2, is the Thomistic "principle of causality.") Obviously there is nothing in this that entails that God would have to have a cause, since God is supposed to have always existed as a necessary being. Whether one thinks the Second Way ultimately works or not, it does not commit the simple and obvious fallacy of which popular accounts of the argument sometimes accuse it.

It has also sometimes been claimed (for example by Anthony Kenny) that Aquinas's proofs rest on outdated Aristotelian scientific theory, and thus are irrelevant in the present day. But as noted in chapter 2, Aristotle's metaphysics stands or falls independently of his physics, and as we shall see, while the Five Ways definitely presuppose certain Aristotelian metaphysical claims, there is never a point in any of the arguments where appeal need be made to now falsified theories in physics or any of the other sciences. Indeed, we will see that the Five Ways remain as interesting and worthy of consideration today as any other philosophical argument.

The First Way

As presented in the *Summa Theologiae*, the proof from motion goes as follows. We know from experience that "some things are in motion" ("motion" in the Aristotelian sense just being change, as we saw in our discussion of Aristotle's reply to Parmenides). Now motion or change is just the reduction of something from potentiality to actuality. But "nothing can be reduced from potentiality to actuality except by something in a state of actuality" (*ST* I.2.3); for instance, fire, which is actually hot, makes wood, which is otherwise only potentially hot, become actually hot. Moreover, nothing can be both potential and actual in the same respect at the same time; what is actually hot, for example, is not at the same time potentially hot, but potentially cold. In that case, though, it is impossible for anything to be at the same time and in the same respect both that which is moved or changed and that which does the moving or changing. Hence, "whatever is in motion must be put in motion by another" (*ST* I.2.3). By the same token, if that which puts something else in motion is itself moving, there must be yet something further moving *it*, and so on. But if such a series went on to infinity, then there would be no first mover; and if there were no first mover, there would be no other movers, for "subsequent movers move only inasmuch as they are put in motion by the first mover; as the staff moves only because it is put in motion by the hand" (*ST* I.2.3). It follows that "it is necessary to arrive at a first mover, put in motion by no other; and this everyone understands to be God" (*ST* I.2.3).

To begin at the end, someone might immediately object to this argument that whatever else Aquinas has shown, he hasn't really shown that such a "first mover" would be God, if by God we mean a being that can be said to be all powerful, all knowing, all good, and the like. There are two things to be said in reply. First, what Aquinas is getting at in the last line of the proof is that whatever else God is supposed to be, he is supposed to be the ultimate explanation of why things happen in the world; hence, if it can be proved that there is a being who explains this, it follows that at least to that extent it will have been proved that there is something in reality corresponding to our idea of God. And he is surely right about that much. Second, while we do of course also want to know why we should regard such a being as all-powerful, all-knowing, all-good, and so forth, as I have said before, Aquinas does in fact answer that question in great detail later on in the *Summa* (and elsewhere). We will see how he does so after first looking at each of the Five Ways.

The question for now, then, is this: does this argument really establish the existence of a first Unmoved Mover? Note first of all that the argument cannot be criticized by appealing to a variation on the standard "If everything has a cause, then what caused God?" objection. Aquinas does not say that everything is in motion, but only that "some things" are in motion; nor does he say that everything is moved by something else, but only that "whatever is in motion" is moved by something else. Hence it will not do to ask "Doesn't that mean that God must be in motion?" or "What moves God, then?" For there is nothing in Aquinas's premises that implies that God would have to be changing like everything else is, or that he must be moved by something else.

What, then, of this key premise of the argument, that is, that "whatever is in motion must be put in motion by another"? The bulk of the proof is devoted to supporting it. Yet it has often been suggested that Aquinas's argument for it fails. One common objection is that the activity of animals shows that the premise is simply false. For isn't it just obvious that animals move themselves? But as we noted in chapter 2, Aquinas does not deny that there is a loose sense in which animals move themselves. Strictly speaking, though, when an animal moves this only occurs because one part of the animal moves another part, as when the legs of a dog move because of the flexing of its muscles, the muscles flex only because of the firing of certain motor neurons, and so forth. When considered in detail, then, the example of animal movement does not constitute a counterexample to the principle that "whatever is moved is moved by another."

It is also sometimes alleged that Aquinas is committed to the principle that whatever causes something actually to be *F* must itself actually be *F*, and that this principle is clearly false. For he gives the example of wood being made to catch fire by something which is already on fire; but as Kenny points out, fire could also be generated instead by taking two sticks that are not already on fire, and rubbing them together. But there are two problems with this objection. First, it ignores the possibility that Aquinas is here appealing to what we called in chapter 2 the "principle of proportionate causality," according to which whatever is in an effect must somehow be in its cause, but where this allows that the cause might have the relevant feature "virtually" or "eminently" rather than "formally." In other words, Aquinas is not making the obviously false claim that only what is already on fire can cause fire; he is rather making the claim (perfectly defensible, as we saw in the previous chapter) that whatever causes fire must have an inherent power to cause it. Second, as many commentators have pointed out, Aquinas is probably not relying in this argument on any version of the principle in question in the first place. That is, he is not saying that "whatever causes something actually to be F must itself be F in some way," but rather that "whatever causes something must itself be actual," that nothing merely potential can cause anything. As Rudi te Velde has suggested, some critics place too much significance on the physical details of the examples Aquinas gives in the course of the proof, failing to see that their point is merely to illustrate certain basic metaphysical principles rather than to support broad empirical or quasi-scientific generalizations.

Thus understood, what Aquinas is saying here is essentially just what we have already noted him saying in developing the distinction between act and potency, namely that no potency or potential can actualize itself, precisely because it is merely potential and not actual. Hence only what is itself already actual can actualize a given potency, and therefore (given that motion is just the actualization of a potency) "whatever is moved is moved by another." This is not some dubious conjecture based on the observation of how wood catches fire and the like; it is rather supposed to be a metaphysical certainty the denial of which would be conceptually incoherent. Indeed, the principle in question is but a variation on what we referred to in chapter 2 as the "principle of causality," which we have seen to be eminently defensible.

So far, so good, then. But what about the claim that a series of movers could not go on to infinity? Isn't Aquinas just begging the question (arguing in a circle) when he asserts that if there were no first mover then there would be no movers at all? For why could there not be an infinite series of movers, so that no matter how far back you go in the series, you could always go back to yet another mover? In that case it seems there would be an explanation for the motion of any member of the series you care to take, without having to appeal to a first mover.

But in fact Aquinas is not begging the question at all, and has good reason for claiming that such a series could not go on to infinity. Keep in mind first of all that the proof from motion, like all the Five Ways, is not an attempt to show that the universe had a beginning at some point in the past and that God must have caused that beginning. Aquinas is not saying that if you trace the series of movers back in time you must eventually get to some temporally first mover. As we saw in chapter 2, for Aquinas as for Aristotle, the immediate cause of an effect is *simultaneous* with that effect: "It is clear that when a thing moves because it is moved, the mover and the mobile object are moved simultaneously" (*In Phys* VII.2.892). So the series of movers he has in mind is one all of whose members exist together *here and now* (and at any moment we might be considering the argument), and by saying that there must be a first mover, he doesn't mean first in order of time, but rather first in the sense of being most fundamental in the order of what exists.

This brings us to an important distinction Aquinas and other medieval thinkers made between two kinds of series of efficient causes. On the one hand there are causal series ordered *per accidens* or "accidentally," in the sense that the causal activity of any particular member of the series is not essentially dependent on that of any prior member of the series. Take, for example, the series consisting of Abraham begetting Isaac, Isaac begetting Jacob, and Jacob begetting Joseph. Once he has himself been begotten by Abraham (and then grows to maturity, of course), Isaac is fully capable of begetting Jacob on his own, even if Abraham dies in the meantime. It is true that he would not have existed had Abraham not begotten him, but the point is that once Isaac exists he has the power to beget a son all by himself, and Abraham's continued existence or non-existence is irrelevant to his exercise of that power. The same is true of Jacob with respect to both Abraham and Isaac, and of Joseph with respect to Abraham, Isaac, and Jacob. Given that we are considering them as a series of begetters specifically, each member is independent of the others as far as its causal powers are concerned. Contrast this with a causal series ordered per se or "essentially." Aquinas's example from the First Way of the staff which is moved by the hand is a standard illustration, and we can add to the example by supposing that the staff is being used to move a stone, which is itself moving a fallen leaf. Here the motion of the leaf depends essentially on the motion of the stone, which in turn depends essentially on the motion of the staff, which itself depends essentially in turn on the motion of the hand. For if any member higher up in the series ceases its causal activity, the activity of the lower members will necessarily cease as well. For instance, if the staff was to slip away from the stone, the stone, and thus the leaf too, will stop moving; and of course, if the hand stops moving, the whole series, staff included, will automatically stop. In this case the causal power of the lower members derives entirely from that of the first member, the hand. In fact, strictly speaking it is not the stone which is moving the leaf and the staff which is moving the stone, but rather the hand which is moving everything else, with the stone being used by it as an instrument to move the leaf and the staff being used as an instrument to move both stone and leaf.

Causal series ordered *per accidens* are linear in character and extend through time, as in the begetting example, in which Abraham's begetting Isaac occurs well before Isaac's begetting Jacob, and Isaac's begetting Jacob occurs well before Jacob's begetting Joseph. Causal series ordered per se are paradigmatically hierarchical with their members acting simultaneously, as in the staff example where the movement of the leaf occurs precisely when the movement of the stone occurs, which is precisely when the movement of the staff occurs, which is precisely when the movement of the hand occurs. Now it is in Aquinas's view at least theoretically possible for a causal series ordered *per accidens* to regress to infinity, and thus have no beginning point (*ST* I.46.2). (This is why Aquinas thinks it is not possible to prove via purely philosophical arguments that the world must have had a beginning in time.) For since each member of such a series has its causal power independently of the earlier members, there is no need to trace any particular member's action back to the activity of a first member; for instance, when Jacob begets Joseph, it is precisely Jacob who begets him, and not Abraham who begets him by using Isaac and Jacob as instruments. By contrast, "in efficient causes it is impossible to proceed to infinity per se – thus, there cannot be an infinite number of causes that are per se required for a certain effect; for instance, that a stone be moved by a stick, the stick by the hand, and so on to infinity" (*ST* I.46.2). For "that which moves as an instrumental cause cannot move unless there be a principal moving cause" (*SCG* I.13.15). That is to say, since the lower members of a causal series ordered per se have no causal power on their own but derive it entirely from a first cause, which (as it were) uses them as instruments, there is no sense to be made of such a series having no first member. If a first member who is the source of the causal power of the others did not exist, the series as a whole simply would not exist, as the movement of the leaf, stone, and staff cannot occur in the absence of the hand.

What Aquinas is saying, then, is that it is in the very nature of causal series ordered per se to have a first member, precisely because everything else in the series only counts as a member in the first place relative to the actions of a first cause. To suggest that such a series might regress infinitely, without a first member, is therefore simply unintelligible. The leaf is "moved" by the stone only in a loose sense; strictly speaking, the leaf, stone, and staff are all really being moved by the hand. Thus to suggest that this series of purely instrumental causes might regress to infinity is incoherent, for they would not in that case be the instruments *of* anything at all (*CT* I.3). As A. D. Sertillanges put it, you might as well say "that a brush can paint by itself, provided it has a very long handle" (quoted by Garrigou-Lagrange in *God: His Existence and His Nature*).

Given their essentially instrumental character, all causes in such a series other than the first cause are referred to by Aquinas as "second causes" ("second" not in the sense of coming after the first but before the third member of the series, but rather in the sense having their causal power only in a secondary or derivative way). It is worth emphasizing that it is precisely this instrumental nature of second causes, the dependence of whatever causal power they have on the causal activity of the first cause, that is the key to the notion of a causal series per se. That the members of such a series exist simultaneously, and that the series does not regress to infinity, are of secondary importance. As Patterson Brown and John Wippel point out, even if a series of causes ordered per se could somehow be said to regress to infinity, it would remain the case, given that they are merely instrumental causes, that there must then be something outside the entire infinite series that imparts to them their causal power.

Whether or not the series of causes *per accidens* regresses infinitely into the past, then – and again, while Aquinas believed that it did not, he didn't think this could be proven through philosophical arguments – a causal series per se existing here and now, and at any moment we are considering the matter, must necessarily trace back to a first member. But strictly speaking, even the hand in Aquinas's example doesn't count as a first mover – the example is intended merely as a first approximation to the notion of a first mover – because it is itself being moved insofar as its activity depends on the motion of the arm, the flexing of certain muscles, and so forth. To understand the way in which such a series regresses and how it *does* and must terminate, it is crucial to remember that for Aquinas, motion or change is just the reduction of potency to act. So when we talk about one thing being moved by another, which is moved by another, and so on, in a causal series ordered per se, this is shorthand for saying that a certain potency is reduced to act by something whose potency is itself reduced to act by something whose potency is itself reduced to act by ... and so forth. (Or, to soften the technical terminology slightly, a certain potentiality is actualized by something whose potentiality is itself actualized by something whose potentiality is itself actualized by ... and so on.) As should be evident, such a series can only possibly terminate in something which is not reduced to act or actualized by anything else, but which just *is* in act or actual, and thus "unmoving." The potential of the hand for movement is actualized here and now by the flexing of the muscles of the hand, the potential of the muscles to flex is actualized here and now by the firing of certain motor neurons, the potential of the motor neurons to fire is actualized here and now by the firing of certain other neurons, and so forth. Eventually this regress must terminate in something which here and now actualizes potentialities without itself being actualized, an unmoved mover.

Now Kenny objects that the notion of an unmoved mover merely gives us something at rest, like a stationary billiard ball, and thus seems hardly relevant to proving the existence of God. But as Garrigou-Lagrange points out, and as should be clear from our discussion thus far, an unmoved mover of the sort we've been describing is not and cannot be "unmoved" in the sense of being in repose, precisely because it is that which actualizes the potencies of second causes. It is *active*, not "at rest." There is still a further question, however. Even if it is granted that the First Way takes us to an *unmoved* mover, why should we hold (as Aquinas does) that this mover is also *unmovable*? As Scott MacDonald suggests, it may be that a first mover of the sort whose existence is established by Aquinas's argument is one that is *capable* of motion even if, qua first mover, it does not *in fact* move. In other words, for all Aquinas has shown, a first mover may well *have* certain potencies which are not in fact being *actualized*, at least not insofar as it is functioning as the first mover in some series of efficient causes ordered per se. Perhaps its potencies are actualized at some other time, when it is not so functioning; or perhaps they never are. But as long as it has them, it will not be something that can be characterized as "pure act," and thus, given Aquinas's own commitments, it will not be identifiable with God. To get to a first mover of pure act, and thus one which is truly unmovable, would require in MacDonald's view some further argument, in which case the argument from motion could succeed as an argument for God's existence only by being "parasitic" on such a further argument.

Yet MacDonald is, I think, mistaken. Consider how the series we have been describing would have to continue beyond the point at which we left it, with the hand's potentiality for motion actualized by the arm, the arm's potentiality for motion actualized by the flexing of certain muscles, the muscles' potentiality for flexing actualized by the firing of certain motor neurons, and so on and so forth, all simultaneously. All of this depends in turn on the overall state of the nervous system, which depends on its molecular structure, which depends on the atomic basis of that molecular structure, which depends on electromagnetism, gravitation, the weak and strong forces, and so on and so forth, all simultaneously, all here and now. That the molecules composing the nervous system constitute a nervous system specifically amounts to their having a certain potency which is here and now actualized, that the atoms composing the molecules constitute just those molecules amounts to their having a certain potency which is simultaneously actualized, and so on. To account for the reduction of potency to act in the case of the *operations or activities* of the hand, the muscles, and so on, we are led ultimately to appeal to the reduction of potency to act vis-à-vis the *existence or being* of ever deeper and more general features of reality; for "it is evident that anything whatever operates so far as it is a being" (*QDA* 19). But the only way to stop this regress and arrive at a first member of the series is with something whose very existence, and not merely its operations or activities, need not be actualized by anything else. This would just be something which, since it simply exists without being made to exist by anything, or is actual without being actualized, is pure act, with no admixture of potentiality whatsoever. For suppose it had some potency relevant to its existence (its existence being what is relevant to its status as the end of the regress as we have continued it). Then either some other thing actualizes that potency, in which case we haven't really stopped the regress after all, contrary to hypothesis; or some already actual part of it actualizes the potency, in which case that already actual part would *itself* be both pure act and, properly speaking, the true first mover. Now, having no potency to actualize, such a being could not possibly change or move. Thus we have reached a first mover that is not only unmoved, but unmovable.

MacDonald might object to this that the move from accounting for the activities or operations of things to accounting for their existence or being in effect involves an appeal to something other than motion, and thus to an argument other than the argument from motion; and though (as MacDonald would acknowledge) this would not by itself show that there is anything wrong with the argument, it would leave untouched his claim that the First Way by itself is incomplete and "parasitic" for any effectiveness it has vis-à-vis proving God's existence on some other argument. But as commentators like Norman Kretzmann and D. Q. McInerny have noted, if the point of an argument from motion is to explain motion, and to explain motion requires explaining the existence of the things doing the moving and the way in which factors outside them contribute to their ability to move, then an explanation of the existence of moving things is quite naturally going to be a part of any argument from motion. More to the point, if motion is just the reduction of potency to act, then since the existence of a thing no less than its activity involves (in everything other than that which is pure act) the reduction of potency to act, any explanation of motion must account for the existence of things and not just their activities. Far from making an argument from motion "parasitic" on some other kind of argument, the move to the explanation of the existence of moving things is a necessary part of any such argument.

Notice that at no point in our exposition of the argument from motion have we had to appeal to any claims from Aristotelian physics, "outmoded" or otherwise. The argument proceeds entirely in terms of such metaphysical notions as the act/potency distinction, the principle of causality, and so forth. Still, it is sometimes suggested that Newton's principle of inertia undermines the proof from motion, for if (as that principle tells us) it is just a law of physics that a body in motion tends to stay in motion unless acted upon from outside, then (so it is claimed) Aquinas's view that whatever is moving must here and now be moved by something else is thereby shown to be false. But there are several problems with this objection. First and most obviously, Newton's principle concerns only "local motion" or movement from one place to another, while motion in the Aristotelian sense includes (as we have seen) not just local motion, but also changes in quality (like water becoming solid when it freezes), changes in quantity (as when a pool of water gets larger or smaller), and changes in substance (as when hydrogen and oxygen are combined to make water) (*In Phys* III.2.286). (There is a strict sense of "motion" within the Aristotelian tradition on which changes in substance are not counted as motions, but they are motions or changes in a loose sense; and as several commentators have noted, they do in any case count as reductions of potency to act of the sort the argument from motion seeks to account for.) At the very least, then, the defender of the First Way can say that whether or not local motion needs an explanation of the sort the argument provides, these other kinds of change do need such an explanation.

But in fact there is no good reason to exclude local motion from the range of that which needs explanation in terms of a first unmoved mover. After all, it is no good just to say "Well, it's simply a law of physics that things in motion tend to stay in motion unless acted upon from outside." For one thing, there is still the question of what puts something in motion in the first place, and in general of a thing's acquisition or loss of momentum, and explaining these events will require just the sort of explanation the First Way tells us other instances of change do. More fundamentally, we also still need to know *what it is* exactly for something to be a law of physics, and *why* such a law holds.

Regarding the first question, some defenders of the First Way have suggested that Newton's principle is nothing more than a mathematical model which is of utility in making predictions but which strictly speaking does not describe the objective nature of physical objects. One reason for adopting such an instrumentalist (as opposed to realist) interpretation of the principle of inertia is that to interpret the principle realistically would commit us (so it is argued) to the metaphysically absurd consequence that a finite cause can have an infinite effect. It is then sometimes further suggested that to explain local motion, especially of a projectile sort, we need therefore to postulate that the initial cause of a thing's movement (the arm which throws a spear, say) imparts to it a force, "impulse," or "impetus" which keeps it in motion, and thus passing from potency to act, as long as it does move, and where this impetus serves as an instrumental cause whose efficacy must ultimately be traced to the simultaneous activity of a first mover. Other defenders of the argument reject this "impetus" theory and would grant that Newton's principle does tell us something about the real nature of physical objects. But they would then insist that this simply leaves us with the question of what actualizes the potential existence of things having natures of the sort described by the principle of inertia, and that to answer this question we have (for reasons already seen) to appeal to something which is pure act. In short, Newton's principle can hardly undermine the First Way if the existence of a first unmovable mover is needed in order to explain why the principle holds in the first place.

But it may be that even these general points concede too much force to the objection, for things are much less conceptually clear cut here than it might at first appear. For example, if, as is standardly done, we think of Newtonian inertial motion as a "state" rather than a process, then we need to get clear on exactly how such "motion" could be motion in the Aristotelian sense (i.e. a genuine *change*), in which case it also needs to be made clear exactly how Newton's principle is supposed to conflict with the Aristotelian principle that what is in motion (that is, changing) requires a mover. Or if inertial motion *is* change of some sort, then we need to get clear on the sense in which such motion can be said to be a "state." It should also be kept in mind that in the physical universe as it actually exists, no object undergoing local motion is ever unaffected by outside forces, given for example the constant gravitational attraction every body exerts on every other. Hence at every moment at which an object is moving through space, and not merely at its initial acquisition of momentum, its motion is being affected in a way that requires explanation in terms of something outside it. But in that case, even with respect to the explanation of local motion, the principle of inertia seems practically moot. The conceptual waters here are deep, and reflect difficulties for interpreting modern physics that arise *whatever* its relationship to Aristotelian metaphysics. The point is that those who assert a conflict between Aquinas and Newton simply have not made their case until they have worked out these crucial details. It will not do lazily to assert, without addressing these issues, that modern physics has somehow "explained" local motion in such a way that reference to a first mover is unnecessary.

Another objection sometimes raised against the First Way is that anything moving something else, including a first mover, would have to be undergoing motion itself, as for example the hand of our example moves even as it is moving the staff. Therefore (the objection continues) the very notion of an unmoved mover is incoherent. But this objection begs the question. The argument from motion claims to prove that no motion, including the motion of moved movers, would be possible at all unless there is a first mover which is pure act and thus unmovable. So, given that the premises of this argument are true and that the conclusion follows logically from them, it follows that the conclusion is true and therefore coherent. Accordingly, it won't do simply to insist that the conclusion must be false; one has to show specifically either that one of the premises is false or that the conclusion does not follow. Otherwise, one ought to admit that the argument shows precisely that an unmoved mover really is possible (since actual) after all.

Besides, it is hardly as if the notion of an unmoved mover were anything like as problematic as that of (say) an "immortal mortal." An "immortal mortal" would be something that both dies and does not die, which is self-contradictory. But an unmoved mover is something that makes other things move without itself undergoing motion, and there is no *obvious* self-contradiction in that. Furthermore, as G. H. Joyce argues, the reason that the movers of our experience are themselves moving even as they move other things is precisely because they are limited in the various ways entailed by being composites of act and potency. (For example, because an arm is actually at one point in space and only potentially at another, its potential to be at some other point in space has to be actualized by something else if it is to get the staff to that other point in space.) But something which is pure act, devoid of all potency, would have no such limitations, and thus not need to be moved itself as it is moving other things. Moreover, it would (as we shall see later) be outside of time, and indeed that which creates time, so that to the extent that the objection in question implicitly assumes that the first mover goes from not acting at one moment in time to acting at another moment in time, the objection simply misconceives the nature of the first mover's activity (*In Phys* VIII.2.989). Finally, as Garrigou-Lagrange points out, given that (as we will see a little later on) our knowledge of the first mover is necessarily largely negative, it should not be surprising if it is harder for us to get our minds around it than it is for us to understand the more mundane movers of our experience.

We have devoted a good deal of space to the First Way, partly because of its intrinsic importance and partly because Aquinas himself put so much emphasis on it. (He famously regarded it as the "more manifest way" [*ST* I.2.3] and presented versions of the argument from motion again and again in his writings, as the citations given above indicate.) Moreover, many of the issues that arise in the discussion of the First Way, such as the impossibility of an infinite regress of causes ordered per se, also arise in discussion of the other ways. Hence our fairly detailed discussion of the First Way helps to set the stage for our treatment of the others. Most importantly, it has also (hopefully) shown that the objections commonly raised against the argument are hardly as conclusive as they are sometimes assumed to be, and that it is, accordingly, as worthy of consideration today as it was in Aquinas's day.

The Second Way

The proof from causality begins by noting that the senses reveal to us an order of efficient causes. But nothing can be the cause of itself, for if it were then "it would be prior to itself, which is impossible" (ST I.2.3). Now in a series of efficient causes, the first cause is the cause of the intermediate cause or causes, which are in turn the cause of the ultimate cause. So if there were no first cause, then there would be no intermediate or ultimate causes at all (and thus no causes of the sort we started out acknowledging that we know through the senses). But if the series of efficient causes regressed to infinity, then there would be no first cause. Hence the series cannot go on to infinity, and "therefore it is necessary to admit a first efficient cause, to which everyone gives the name of God" (ST I.2.3).

Let us note first (and yet again) that Aquinas does *not* say, here or elsewhere, that "everything has a cause"; rather, he begins the argument by saying that there are efficient causes and that nothing can cause itself. The implication is that if something is caused, then it is something outside the thing being caused that is doing the causing; and as we have seen in chapter 2, Aquinas is committed in particular to the principle of causality, according to which *that which comes into being*, or more generally *that which is contingent*, must have a cause. Needless to say, this is not the same thing as to claim that *everything* without exception has a cause. So the argument is in no way vulnerable to the stock objection aimed at the stock caricature of cosmological arguments (i.e. "If everything has a cause, then what caused God?"). We have also already seen in chapter 2 how the principle of causality might be defended against the sorts of objections raised by Hume.

There is another sort of objection to the principle of causality, however, or at least to the application made of it by arguments like the Second Way. According to Immanuel Kant (1724–1804), the principle of causality applies only to the world of sensory experience and cannot take us beyond it to a transcendent first cause. As usually presented, however, this objection seems little more than a dogmatic refusal even to consider the possibility of a proof for a first cause; certainly no one who does not accept Kant's highly controversial conception of the nature and limits of human knowledge has any reason to take it seriously. More to the point, as Maurice Holloway argues, from the fact that our knowledge of the principle of causality derives from our experience of sensible things (i.e. things which can be sensed), it simply doesn't follow that it cannot be applied beyond the realm of sensory experience. For the principle applies to sensible things themselves not insofar as they are sensible, but rather insofar as they exist. In particular, a stone, tree, or human being stands in need of a cause not by virtue of being a sensible object, but rather by virtue of being something to whose essence an act of existing must be conjoined if it is to be real. Yet, as even most non-Thomists would acknowledge, the notion of existence is broader than the notion of the sensible; certainly there is no difficulty making sense of the idea of non-sensible existing things given Aquinas's doctrine of analogy, the transcendentals, and so on. Hence there is no reason to doubt that the principle of causality applies beyond the realm of sensible things. At any rate, simply to insist, on the basis of some non-Thomistic epistemology (e.g. a Kantian epistemology) that it cannot apply to non-sensible things, merely begs the question against Aquinas.

It should be obvious that the reason Aquinas rules out the possibility of an infinite regress of causes in the Second Way is the same as the reason he rules out the possibility of an infinite regress of movers in the First Way. What he has in mind, here as there, is a causal series ordered per se, not a causal series ordered *per accidens*; and his point, accordingly, is not that the universe must have had a beginning in time, but rather that whether or not it has always existed, it must here and now be sustained by a first uncaused cause. Hence, the points made in exposition of the First Way vis-à-vis infinite causal regresses apply here as well.

Indeed, it might seem that the two arguments differ little except verbally, the one making reference to motion, the other to efficient causes, but in substance more or less saying the same thing (especially given that moving or changing something just is an instance of efficient causation). But of course, the fact that Aquinas bothers to present them as distinct arguments at all is a clue that there must be more than a verbal difference between them (otherwise he could have stopped with four ways rather than five). Some commentators have suggested that the substantive difference between them is that the First Way seeks to explain how the things of our experience are capable of being passive recipients of change, while the Second Way seeks to explain how they can be active agents of change. But this seems questionable given that the First Way speaks not only of how some things undergo change, but also of how other things can cause change (even if only by being instruments of the first cause), and that the Second Way speaks not only of how things can cause change, but also of how they are being caused. A more plausible and interesting account of the difference between the arguments is provided by Etienne Gilson, who suggests that whereas the First Way is concerned to explain why things undergo change, the Second Way is intended to explain why they exist at all, where (as in the First Way) the causal influence of the first cause is not something that occurred merely at some point in the past, but which exists here and now. That is to say, just as the First Way is meant to show that no motion or change would occur here and now unless there were a first unmoved mover operating here and now, the Second Way is meant to show that nothing would even exist here and now unless there were a first uncaused cause sustaining things in being here and now.

One way to understand this interpretation is in terms of an argument for God's existence that Aquinas presents in chapter 4 of *On Being and Essence*, and which is sometimes called "the existential proof" or "the existence argument." Recall that for Aquinas, in everything other than God, essence is distinct from existence. (This isn't to assume from the outset that God exists, an assumption which would of course make the argument that follows a circular one; the point is just that *if* there is a God – which at this stage of the argument is yet to be determined – in him alone essence and existence would be identical.) So, how does a thing come into existence? That is to say, how is its essence conjoined with an act of existence so that it is made real? "It is impossible," Aquinas says, "that the act of existing itself be caused by the form or quiddity – and by 'caused' I mean as by an efficient cause – for then something would be the cause of itself and produce itself in existence, which is impossible" (*DEE* 4). In other words, a thing's essence, form, or quiddity cannot be what brings the thing into existence, for considered by itself an essence is merely potential, and thus cannot cause anything. For an essence to be able to cause something it would first have to be actualized by being conjoined to an act of existing, and that would entail that the thing itself (since it just is a composite of an essence with an act of existing) would already exist. Hence the essence of a thing could cause its existence only if the thing already existed, in which case the thing would in effect be bringing itself into existence, which is incoherent. "It is therefore necessary that everything whose act of existing is other than its nature have its act of existing from another" (*DEE* 4). But a series of things deriving their acts of existing from something else cannot go on to infinity. Hence "everything which exists through another is reduced to that which exists through itself, as to a first cause" and "there must be something which causes all things to exist, inasmuch as it is subsistent existence alone" (*DEE* 4). That is, there must be something whose essence and existence are identical, and this we call God.

Keep in mind that a thing's essence and act of existing are distinct not just before it exists, but always, even after they are conjoined so as to make the thing real. (To put a handle on to a brush so as to make a broom doesn't make the handle identical to the brush; neither does conjoining an essence and an act of existence make *them* identical.) Hence it is not enough for a thing to be real that its essence and act of existing be conjoined merely at some point in the past; the essence and act of existing must be *kept* together at every point at which the thing exists. Accordingly, a thing must be caused to exist not once for all, but *continuously*, here and now as well as at the time it first came into being; to use the traditional theological language, it must be *conserved* in existence from moment to moment. But if what conserves it in existence were something which itself was a composite of essence and existence, then that conserving cause would need to be conserved as well. Insofar as the existence of a thing in whom essence and existence are distinct might involve a series of causes, then, we are once again talking about a causal series ordered per se, and thus (as Aquinas says) a causal series which necessarily depends on a first member which is not conserved by anything, but simply exists. In the nature of the case, this could only be something whose essence and existence are not distinct (and thus in need of being conjoined) but identical.

There are obvious affinities between this "existential proof" and the Second Way. Both are concerned with accounting for the existence of things here and now, both reject the notion that a thing could cause itself, and both argue that a series of efficient causes must terminate in a first cause. It is natural to suppose that Aquinas intended in the Second Way to summarize the argument from *On Being and Essence*. But William Lane Craig argues that reasoning of the sort represented by the "existential proof" cannot be smoothly assimilated to the Second Way, for two reasons. First, the Second Way is supposed to take as its starting point causal chains that are evident to the senses, but the conjoining of an essence to an act of existence is not something we can observe. Second, in Aquinas's view only God can possibly conjoin an essence and an act of existing, so that the question of a series of causes, whether infinite or finite, cannot even arise for an "existential proof" style of argument; for God's causal activity in this case would have to be direct rather than instrumental (*ST* I.45.5). Accordingly, for Craig the Second Way must be interpreted as concerned with more mundane respects in which one thing causes, here and now, the existence of another, such as the way in which your existence is here and now dependent in part on the temperature of the earth's atmosphere, which is in turn dependent on the earth's distance from the sun, and so on.

Yet Craig's suggestion is not altogether convincing. For one thing, it would be very odd, especially given the centrality of Aquinas's doctrine of essence and existence to his metaphysical system in general and to his conception of God in particular, if he left the argument of *On Being and Essence* off his list of the Five Ways in which he says God's existence can be proved; and the Second Way is the closest of the Five Ways to the argument of *On Being and Essence*. (The Third Way, as we shall see, does deal with the distinction between contingent and necessary beings, but for Aquinas this doesn't correspond to the distinction between beings in which essence and existence are distinct and beings in which they are identical.) Moreover, though Craig correctly notes that Aquinas believes that only God can conjoin essence and existence, this did not stop Aquinas himself from raising the issue of a series of causes in the course of giving the "existential proof" in *On Being and Essence*; in particular, he says that a first cause of the being of things is necessary, for "otherwise we would proceed to infinity in causes" (*DEE* 4), which, again, parallels the argument of the Second Way. Perhaps he did so purely "for the sake of argument"; that is to say, Aquinas may have meant to say only that even if there were a series of causes involved in the conjoining of the essence and existence of a thing (which he did not in fact think there is), such a series would still have to have a first member. But if the notion of a series of causes was indeed being raised in the "existential proof" in this purely "for the sake of argument" manner, perhaps that is also the spirit in which Aquinas meant to raise it in the Second Way. Finally, while the Second Way does indeed explicitly begin with what is evident to the senses, so too does the First Way, in its appeal to the fact of motion; and yet the First Way also almost immediately makes a transition into metaphysics insofar as it analyzes motion in terms of act and potency. It does not seem unreasonable to suppose that in the Second Way too, though Aquinas begins with something evident to the senses, namely the fact that things are caused to exist, the rest of the argument is to be read in terms of the metaphysical analysis of a thing's existence as something that needs to be conjoined with its essence if the thing is to be real. This would certainly make it easier to understand why a first cause would have to be itself uncaused: it could not fail to be if its essence and existence are identical, and thus in no need of being conjoined by a yet further cause.

It seems plausible, then, to read the Second Way in light of the "existential proof" of *On Being and Essence*, an argument which Thomists have in any event always considered extremely important to a proper understanding of Aquinas's conception of God, his relationship to the world, and the grounds of our knowledge of his existence. And whether they are more or less the same argument or not, they both certainly bring into focus Aquinas's view that the way in which philosophy can reveal to us the existence of a divine creator is *not* by proving that God must have caused the world to exist at some point in the past (which of course would raise the question of whether he still exists), but rather by proving that God must be sustaining the world in being here and now, and at any moment in which we are considering the question of his existence. As Peter Geach puts it, for Aquinas the claim that God made the world "is more like 'the minstrel made music' than 'the blacksmith made a shoe'"; that is to say, creation is an ongoing activity rather than a once-and-for-all event. While the shoe might continue to exist even if the blacksmith dies, the music necessarily stops when the minstrel stops playing, and the world would necessarily go out of existence if God stopped creating it.

These considerations should make it clear why an objection to "first cause" arguments famously raised by Hume (and distinct from his criticism of the principle of causality) has no force against Aquinas's argument. If we have explained each member of a causal series by appealing to an earlier member, what need, Hume asks, do we have for a first cause? For even if we trace the series of causes back infinitely, we will never have a case where any individual thing is left unexplained. As we have seen, if causal series ordered *per accidens* are in question, Aquinas would agree with Hume that no first cause is necessary. But it is causal series ordered per se that the Second Way, like the First Way, is concerned with, and here the need for a first cause follows from the fact that in such a series all causes other than the first cause are purely instrumental, having no causal power of their own at all. Extending the series back to infinity would not change this in the least; as noted in our discussion of the First Way, even if a causal series ordered per se *were* infinitely long, as long as each member of this infinitely long series was purely instrumental, and thus causally inert of itself, there would have to be a cause outside the series which imparted causal power to all of the series' members, a cause which would then be "first" not in the sense of coming at the head of the series, but rather in the sense of being that on which every member of the series depends for its causal power. The irrelevance of Hume's objection is even more obvious when we consider the role played in Aquinas's argument by the distinction between essence and existence. For even if each member in a causal series extending backwards in time was caused by some earlier member, with the series going back infinitely, as long as the existence of each member is distinct from its essence, it will have to be conserved in existence at each moment by a first cause in whom existence and essence are identical. What matters is what causes each member to exist *here and now*; causes existing at previous moments of time, even if they are infinite in number, are totally irrelevant.

Another, related objection to "first cause" arguments is that they allegedly commit the "fallacy of composition." If each brick in a certain wall weighs a pound, it doesn't follow that the wall as a whole weighs a pound; similarly (the objection continues) if each thing in the universe requires a cause, it doesn't follow that the universe as a whole must have a cause. But there are two problems with this objection, at least considered as a criticism of Aquinas. First, as is well known to logicians, part-to-whole reasoning of the sort under consideration is not in fact always fallacious. For example, if every brick in a wall built out of a child's Lego blocks is red, then it follows that the wall as a whole is red. Similarly, given that the distinction between essence and existence suffices to show that any particular material thing requires a cause, it is surely correct to say that the universe as a whole, which is comprised of these material things and which itself has an essence distinct from its existence, must also have a cause. Second, Aquinas's argument does not in fact require reasoning in this part-to-whole fashion in any case. To get the proof from causality going (especially if it is understood in light of the "existential proof") one need not consider the universe as a whole, but just any individual thing whose essence is distinct from its existence – a book, a car, a dog, a tree, whatever. For to explain *even that single thing* will (if Aquinas's argument is otherwise unobjectionable) require appeal to something whose essence and existence are identical, and thus appeal to an uncaused first cause.

The Third Way

The proof from the contingency of the world starts from the fact that there are in the natural order things for which it is possible either to exist or not exist, as is evident from the fact that they are generated and corrupted, coming into being and passing away. But "that which is possible not to be at some time is not" (*ST* I.2.3); that is to say, if it is possible for something not to exist, then at some time it will not exist. "Therefore, if everything is possible not to be, then at one time there could have been nothing in existence" (*ST* I.2.3). Now if there ever were a time when nothing existed, then nothing would exist now, because "that which does not exist only begins to exist by something already existing" (*ST* I.2.3), so that if there was nothing in existence at some point in the past there would have been no way for anything new to be brought into existence. But since it would be absurd to hold that nothing exists now, it follows (given that the assumption that everything that exists is merely possible leads to this absurdity) that not everything that exists is merely possible, that is, capable of either existing or not existing; and therefore "there must exist something the existence of which is necessary" (*ST* I.2.3). Now "every necessary thing either has its necessity caused by another, or not" (*ST* I.2.3). But it is impossible to go on to infinity in a series of necessary things which get their necessity from another, for the reasons already discussed when considering series of efficient causes. Therefore there must be something "having of itself its own necessity, and not receiving it from another, but rather causing in others their necessity" (*ST* I.2.3), and this is what we call God.

In short, the Third Way holds that the world of contingent things could not exist at all unless there were a necessary being. It would be a serious mistake, however, to understand "contingent" and "necessary" here in the senses most familiar to contemporary philosophers, many of whom think (for example) of what is necessary as that which exists in every possible world and of what is contingent as that which exists only in some possible worlds, or who assume that the notion of a necessary being must be that of a being the denial of the existence of which would entail a self-contradiction (thus reading "necessary" as "logically necessary"). As we saw in chapter 2, Aquinas (like other Aristotelian essentialists) would not accept such modern accounts of necessity and contingency.

One common objection to the Third Way which may reflect this misunderstanding is the suggestion that Aquinas commits an obvious fallacy when he claims that "that which is possible not to be at some time is not," for even if it is possible for something to go out of existence, it simply doesn't follow that it will actually do so. This objection would clearly be correct if by "possible not to be" Aquinas meant "non-existent in some possible world" or "the non-existence of which is logically possible," for it is obvious that neither the fact that there is a possible world in which something doesn't exist nor the fact that there is no self-contradiction involved in denying its existence entails anything about its longevity in the actual world. Similarly, it is sometimes claimed against cosmological arguments that only propositions can be necessary, and not things. This too might be a good objection to Aquinas if by "necessary" he meant "logically necessary." But again, Aquinas does not in fact mean "possible" or "necessary" in any of these modern senses, so these objections are irrelevant.

What Aquinas does mean is indicated by the reason he gives for saying that some things are possibly either existent or non-existent, namely that we observe them to be generated and corrupted. Now as we saw in chapter 2, for Aquinas generation and corruption, coming into being and passing away, character-ize the things of our experience because they are composites of form and matter. Their coming to be is just the acquisition by a certain parcel of matter of a certain form, and their passing away is just the loss by a certain parcel of matter of a certain form. Hence it is ultimately this composite, hylemorphic nature that makes it the case that they are "possible to be and not to be" (*ST* I.2.3); it has nothing to do with possible worlds, with there being no self-contradiction involved in denying their existence, or any other such thing. The "possibility" in question is not some abstract logical possibility but rather something "inherent," a tendency "to be corrupted" rooted "in the nature of those things … whose matter is subject to contrariety of forms" (*QDP* 5.3). In other words, given that the matter out of which the things of our experience is composed is always inherently capable of taking on forms different from the ones it happens currently to instanti-ate, these things have a kind of inherent metaphysical instability that guarantees that they will at some point fail to exist. They have no potency or potential for changeless, indefinite existence; hence they cannot exist indefinitely. [3]

By "possible not to be," then, what Aquinas means is something like "having a tendency to stop existing," "inherently transitory," or "impermanent"; and by "necessary" he just means something that is not like this, something that is everlasting, permanent, or non-transitory. Thus there is no fallacy in his inference from "such-and-such is possible not to be" to "such-and-such at some time is not," for this would follow given an Aristotelian understanding of the nature of material substances. Given enough time, such a substance would, if left to itself, *have* to go out of existence eventually. There is no sense to be made of the idea that it might be "possible" for it not to exist and yet that it never in fact goes out of existence no matter how much time passes and even if nothing acts to frustrate its tendency towards corruption, for in that case the claim that it has an inherent tendency towards corruption would be unintelligible. Something that *always* exists would by that very fact show that it is something whose nature does not include any inherent tendency towards corruption, and thus that it is necessary (*In DC* I.29).

However, this still leaves untouched an apparently more serious difficulty with the Third Way. Even if it is granted that Aquinas is justified in holding that whatever is "possible not to be" will at some time go out of existence, it is widely held that his further inference to the effect that if *everything* were "possible not to be" or contingent, then at one time nothing would have existed, is clearly fallacious. Specifically, it is claimed that he is guilty here of a "quantifier shift" fallacy, of inferring from "Everything has some time at which it does not exist" to "There is some time at which everything does not exist." This is called a "quantifier shift" fallacy because the quantifying expression "everything" shifts position from the first statement to the second. That it is a fallacy can be seen by comparing the argument above with parallel arguments that are clearly fallacious. If every student in the room owns a pencil, it does not follow that there is a certain pencil that every student in the room owns; if every human being has someone as a mother, it does not follow that there is someone who is the mother of every human being; and so forth. Similarly, even if every contingent thing goes out of existence at some time, it does not follow that there is some time when they all go out of existence together. An alternative possibility is that even though every contingent thing goes out of existence at some point, there is always at least one other contingent thing that continues to exist in the meantime, and this overlapping series of contingent things could continue on infinitely. (Certainly Aquinas could not rule such an infinite regress out, since it would involve a causal series ordered *per accidens* extending backward in time, and as we have seen, Aquinas concedes for the sake of argument that such a series might not have a first member.) In this case, though, Aquinas's conclusion to the effect that if everything were contingent then nothing would exist now would be blocked, and the Third Way would fail.

But common though this objection is, it is not in fact fatal to Aquinas's argument, for he need not be interpreted as arguing in the fallacious manner described. As several commentators have suggested, what Aquinas really seems to be getting at is the idea that given an infinite stretch of time, and given also the Aristotelian conception of necessity and possibility described above, then if it is even possible for every contingent thing to go out of existence together (which even Aquinas's critic must concede), this possibility must actually come about. For (again, at least given an Aristotelian conception of possibility) it would be absurd to suggest both that it is *possible* for every contingent thing to go out of existence together, and yet that over even an *infinite* amount of time this will never in fact occur. "Possibility" here entails an inherent tendency, which must manifest itself given sufficient time, and an infinite amount of time is obviously more than sufficient. Hence if everything really were contingent, there would have been some time in the past at which nothing existed, in which case nothing would exist now, which is absurd, and so on, and Aquinas's argument would (up to this stage in the proof at least) be vindicated. (Note that it would not help the critic to suggest that the series of contingent things had a beginning in time after all rather than being infinite, for in that case Aquinas could simply say that given the principle of causality this beginning must then have had a cause and that this cause would have to be something non-contingent, i.e. necessary, which is of course what he has been trying to prove the existence of all along.)

At this point the critic of the Third Way might think to challenge the premise that "that which does not exist only begins to exist by something already existing," so as to undermine the claim that if there was ever a time when nothing existed, then nothing would exist now. But this premise is just a variation on the principle of causality, and we have already seen how that principle might be defended. A more promising strategy for the critic might seem to be to suggest (as J. L. Mackie does) that even if individual contingent things all go out of existence, there might still be some underlying stuff out of which they are made (a "permanent stock of matter," in Mackie's words) which persists throughout every generation and corruption. Now if this were so, then what would follow, given the Aristotelian conception of necessity we've been describing, is that this stock of material stuff would itself count as a necessary being. But (so the suggestion continues) the critic could happily accept this (as Mackie does) given that such a "necessary being" would, in view of its material nature, clearly not be divine.

The trouble with this reply, though, is that it falsely purports to be asserting something that Aquinas would deny. In fact, surprising as it might seem, Aquinas would be quite happy, at least for the sake of argument, to concede that the material world as a whole might be a kind of necessary being, in the relevant sense of being everlasting or non-transitory. After all, as we have repeated many times, Aquinas does not think that proving the existence of God requires showing that the material world had a beginning. Moreover, as we noted in our discussion of hylemorphism in chapter 2, Aquinas himself insists that while individual material things are generated and corrupted, matter and form themselves are (apart from special divine creation, to which he would not appeal for the purposes of the argument at hand lest he argue in a circle) not susceptible of generation and corruption. Far from regarding the notion of the material world as necessary as a blow to the project of the Third Way, Aquinas would in fact regard it as a vindication of his claim that there must be a necessary being. Indeed, he recognizes the existence of other non-divine necessary beings as well, such as angels and even heavenly bodies (which, given the astronomical knowledge then available, the medievals mistakenly regarded as not undergoing corruption).

That this should not be surprising, and in particular that it should not be regarded as damaging to the aim of proving the existence of *God* specifically, should be evident when we remember that proving the existence of a necessary being is only one component of the overall argumentative strategy of the Third Way. For recall that at this stage of the argument Aquinas immediately goes on to say that "every necessary thing either has its necessity caused by another, or not" and then argues that a series of necessary beings cannot go on to infinity. This might seem very odd to those contemporary philosophers who think of necessity in terms of possible worlds or who regard all necessity as logical necessity. "How could a necessary being get its necessity from another?" such a philosopher might ask. "It either exists in all possible worlds or it does not, or the assertion of its non-existence either involves a self-contradiction or it does not. End of story. Certainly there can be no question of anything *causing* it to exist in all possible worlds or *causing* it to be logically necessary!" But when we keep in mind that Aquinas does not mean "necessary" in the sense in which such contemporary philosophers understand it, but rather in the sense of "everlast-ing" or "permanent," we can see that it makes perfect sense to consider whether a thing's necessity is derived or not. In partic-ular, we can see that it is not enough to show that the material universe as a whole (or an angel, a heavenly body, or whatever) is a necessary being in the relevant sense. One also needs to know whether it is the sort of thing that could possibly have its necessity in itself, or whether instead it must derive its necessity from something else, from something which *keeps* it in existence everlastingly.

It is immediately obvious, however, that matter qua matter cannot possibly have its necessity of itself, at least on an Aristotelian conception. For matter considered apart from anything else, and in particular apart from form, is just "prime matter" or pure potentiality; and pure potentiality, since by definition it has no actuality, has no reality either, necessary or otherwise. Matter exists only insofar as it is combined with substantial form to comprise a substance. Nor would it help the critic of the Third Way to suggest that it is matter and form together that constitute a necessary being having of itself its own necessity. For one thing, and as we have already noted, individ-ual material things are constantly going out of existence and thus losing their forms, and it is in their nature to do so. Hence it cannot be any particular material substance, but only prime matter, which can be said to be everlasting (and prime matter, for the reasons just given, cannot have its everlastingness of itself). Second, even if there could be some composite of form and matter which exists everlastingly, since in purely material substances form depends on matter just as matter depends on form, we would have (as Martin has pointed out) an explanatory vicious circle unless we appealed to something outside the form/matter composite on which it depends for its existence. Third, since (given Aquinas's doctrine of essence and existence) the existence of any material thing is distinct from its essence, we would need in any case to appeal to something outside it in order to explain how its essence and existence come together so as to make it real. (Note that this particular point would apply to material things even if, contrary to Aristotle and Aquinas, we did not regard them as composites of form and matter.) There is no way, then, plausibly to hold that matter might have its necessity of itself. Even a "necessarily existing" or everlasting material world would have to depend on something outside it for its existence. And this something could not itself be a composite either of form and matter or essence and existence, on pain of infinite regress.

The essence/existence distinction also implies that other sorts of non-divine necessary beings, such as angels (which on Aquinas's view are composites of a pure form together with an act of existing), would have to derive their necessity from something else. The only thing that could stop an explanatory regress of necessary beings would therefore be something whose essence and existence are identical, and who is a necessarily existing being precisely because it just *is* subsistent being or existence. Here we need only refer back to the "existential proof" considered when discussing the Second Way in order to fill in the details; and the upshot is that the Second Way and Third Way appear to converge on exactly the same being, albeit they do so from very different starting points (and thus remain distinct arguments).

One serious weakness of Mackie's otherwise reasonably fair-minded discussion of the Third Way (in the context of what is possibly the best book in philosophy of religion written from an atheistic point of view, *The Miracle of Theism*) is that he never considers the relevance of Aquinas's hylemorphic conception of matter or distinction between essence and existence. Hence he mistakenly concludes that the only way Aquinas could show that the material world itself is not the ultimate necessary being is to transform the Third Way into something like Leibniz's cosmological argument and define a necessary being as one which exists in all possible worlds, or one the non-existence of which would involve a logical self-contradiction, or one whose essence "involves" or "includes" existence. But (to repeat yet again) Aquinas does not mean "necessary" in either the "possible worlds" sense or the logical sense. Nor does he think that a necessary being having its necessity of itself is one whose essence "includes" existence, as if its existence were simply one attribute it had alongside others. Rather, he thinks of it as something which just *is* subsistent existence, Being Itself rather than "a being" among other beings, and (as we shall see later on in this chapter) something absolutely simple or non-composite in which no distinctions can be drawn between its various attributes.

In general, it is remarkable how many critics of the Five Ways almost completely ignore Aquinas's own metaphysical views, and instead read into the arguments all sorts of assumptions that Aquinas himself never made and often would have rejected. It is no wonder, then, that (as we have seen) the objections these critics raise are often wide of the mark. If this is so in the case of the first three Ways, it is perhaps even more so of the last two, to which we turn next.

The Fourth Way

The proof from the grades of perfection begins by noting that "among beings there are some more and some less good, true, noble, and the like" (*ST* I.2.3). But things are said to be "more" or "less" a certain way to the extent that they "resemble" some maximum, "as a thing is said to be hotter according as it more nearly resembles that which is hottest" (*ST* I.2.3). But in that case, it follows that "there is something which is truest, something best, something noblest, and, consequently, something which is uttermost being; for those things that are greatest in truth are greatest in being" (*ST* I.2.3). Now the maximum within any genus is the cause of everything in that genus, "as fire, which is the maximum of heat, is the cause of all hot things" (*ST* I.2.3). So there must be something which is the cause of the "being, goodness, and every other perfection" of all beings, and this is what we call God (*ST* I.2.3).

Of all of the Five Ways, the fourth is generally regarded as the most difficult for modern readers to accept, or even to understand. Even Christopher Martin, whose reading of the other four Ways is very sympathetic, does not claim to understand it, and judges it "strange" or even "bizarre." It seems to me, though, that the mysteriousness of the Fourth Way has been greatly exaggerated, and that while it may well be more out of sync with contemporary philosophers' metaphysical predilections than Aquinas's other proofs, it is perfectly comprehensible and even defensible when properly understood in light of his general metaphysical commitments.

The argument is often said to be among the most Platonic elements of Aquinas's thought, and while it does not in fact presuppose the truth of Platonism, reading it in light of Plato's Theory of Forms does provide at least a useful first approximation to what Aquinas is getting at. For Plato, the ordinary objects of our experience can only be understood in terms of their "resemblance" to or "participation" in ideal archetypes of which they are but imperfect copies. To take a simple example, consider several triangles, some drawn in chalk on a board, some drawn in sand, some drawn on paper in pencil and others in various colors of ink. Now the essence or nature of a triangle is to be a closed plane figure with three straight sides, and it is by reference to this essence that we judge the particular triangles of our example to be triangles in the first place. But notice that each of these particular triangles is going to have certain features that have nothing to do with this essence; for example, some of them will be red and some green, some large and some small, some made out of chalk dust and some out of sand, and so forth, even though there is nothing about triangularity per se that entails any of these features. Notice too that they are all also going to lack, to some extent, some of the features that are part of the essence of a triangle. For instance, some of them will be drawn with partially broken lines or corners that are not perfectly closed, and none will be drawn with lines that are perfectly straight. Moreover, there are certain geometrical truths about triangles, such as that their angles add up to 180 degrees, that are necessary truths in the sense that they would remain true even if every individual material triangle went out of existence. Yet if any material triangle is going to have features that are not part of triangularity and will lack features that are part of it, and if there are truths about triangles that would remain true regardless of whether any material triangles actually exist, then triangularity per se – the essence or archetype by reference to which we judge something to be a more perfect or less perfect instance of a triangle, and indeed to count as a triangle at all – cannot be something material.

Neither, in Plato's view, can it be something mental. For the necessary truths that we know about triangles (such as that their angles add up to 180 degrees, the Pythagorean theorem, etc.) are *objective* truths, something we *discover* rather than invent. We could not change them if we wanted to, and this shows that they do not depend for their existence on our minds. If triangularity as such is neither material nor mental, however, then it has a unique kind of existence of its own, that of an abstract object existing in a "third realm." And what is true of triangles is also true in Plato's view of more or less everything else: of circles, squares, and other geometrical figures; of human beings, dogs, cats, and other living things; of tables, chairs, rocks, trees, and other physical objects; of justice, goodness, beauty, piety, and the like; and so on. When we grasp the essence of any of these things, we grasp something that is *universal* rather than particular (since it is that in virtue of which various individual things count as instances of the same one type), *perfect* rather than imperfect (since it is the pattern or archetype by reference to which we judge something to be more or less perfect), and *eternal* or unchanging (since the truths we know about these essences are necessary truths). For these reasons we also thereby know something that is *more real* than individual particular things, since the latter only have their reality to the extent that they resemble or participate in the former. In short, what we know is what Plato calls a Form.

Now it is easy to see why the Fourth Way would seem to many readers to be Platonic in spirit. Aquinas argues that "'more' and 'less' are predicated of different things, according as they resemble in their different ways something which is the maximum" (*ST* I.2.3), and this "principle of exemplarity" (as Henri Renard has labeled it), with its talk of things "resembling" some maximum more or less perfectly, is certainly reminiscent of Plato. As is well known to scholars of his thought, Aquinas also frequently makes use of the concept of "participation," including in cases where he restates the principle of exemplarity (e.g. *QDP* 3.5, *ST* I.44.1, and *ST* I.79.4), and this concept is clearly Platonic in origin. And unlike the rest of the Five Ways, the Fourth Way seems (at least in its first stage) to be concerned with explaining the world in terms of formal rather than efficient causality (a distinction explained in chapter 2), another apparent departure from Aquinas's usual Aristotelian orientation towards a more Platonic one. The thrust of the argument might therefore seem to be that we can only make sense of the more or less good, true, and noble things of our experience by reference to something like a divine Platonic archetype of goodness, truth, and nobility.

A Platonic reading of the Fourth Way also has the advantage of forestalling an objection commonly heard in these more relativistic times, to the effect that standards of goodness, truth, nobility, and so on are all subjective. For if Platonism is true, then such relativism and subjectivism are no more plausible in the case of goodness and the like than in the case of mathematics. Furthermore, the apparent emphasis on formal rather than efficient causality might seem to explain why Aquinas thinks that the maximum in any genus is the "cause" of everything in that genus. This claim is odd and implausible (so it is said) if Aquinas has efficient causality in mind, but understandable and defensible if he is speaking instead of formal causality.

On the other hand, there is one glaring problem with a Platonic interpretation of the Fourth Way, which is that Aquinas was not a Platonist, but rather an Aristotelian or moderate realist. That is to say, he did not believe in a realm of Forms or abstract objects existing altogether outside the world of concrete objects; as we saw in chapter 2, he took the forms of things to exist instead in the things themselves, and to exist in a universal and abstract way only in the intellect. And as it happens, this moderate realism is (as we shall see in chapter 5) perfectly sufficient to allay any concerns about the purported subjectivity or relativity of standards of goodness and the like; no appeal to Platonism is necessary. Moreover, even if an appeal to formal rather than efficient causality would solve one problem, it would raise another. For being abstract rather than concrete objects, Platonic Forms are causally inert (where efficient causality is concerned); hence if the Fourth Way were really suggesting that we think of God as a kind of Platonic Form, it would be hard to see how the most true, good, and noble being of the Fourth Way could be identical to the First Mover and First Cause of the first two ways.

Then there are certain other objections sometimes raised against the Fourth Way which would seem to be if anything only exacerbated by a Platonic reading. For example, why assume that the most true being, the most good being, and the most noble being are the *same* being? (After all, in Plato's thought each thing's Form is distinct from other Forms.) And given the reasoning of the Fourth Way, wouldn't we have to say that God is not only the most good, true, and noble thing, but also (to quote Dawkins again) the "perfect maximum of conceivable smelliness," and indeed that he possesses to the maximum degree any attribute we can think of? (After all, on Plato's theory, everything has a Form, including not only goodness, truth, and the like, but less elevated and abstract things too, like sweetness, filthiness, illness, and the like.) But this would be absurd, and certainly incompatible with Aquinas's conception of God.

In fact these objections, like others we've examined, rest on egregious misunderstandings of Aquinas's basic metaphysical commitments; and while there are indeed Platonic aspects to the Fourth Way, they are all greatly transformed by Aquinas in light of some of the concepts we surveyed in chapter 2, in a direction more consistent with his general Aristotelianism.

Let us note first that Aquinas is not in fact trying to argue in the Fourth Way that *everything* that we observe to exist in degrees (including heat, smelliness, sweetness, etc.) must be traceable to some single maximum standard of perfection. Here (as elsewhere in the Five Ways) his archaic scientific examples have led modern readers to misread him. Given the (false, we now know) medieval theory that fire is the source of all heat, he naturally appeals to fire and heat merely to *illustrate* the general principle that things that come in degrees point to a maximum. But heat itself is not among the things he is trying here to explain. (This should be obvious when you think about it, since Aquinas would clearly not regard heat or fire as divine attributes!) Rather, he intends to use the principle in question to explain *truth*, *goodness*, *nobility*, *being* and the like specifically. As the reader may have noticed, this list is very similar to the list of "transcendentals" we discussed in chapter 2, which are (unlike heat, smelliness, etc.) above every genus and common to every being, unrestricted to any particular category or individual. And as commentators on the Fourth Way generally recognize, Aquinas is mainly concerned in this argument to show that to the extent that these *transcendental* features of the world come in degrees, they must be traceable to a maximum. (It is true that "nobility" was not on the list of transcendentals we examined in chapter 2, but as Wippel points out, Aquinas's linking of *nobilitas* with being and perfection in *SCG* I.28 indicates that he does not think of it as a transcendental distinct from the others.) Since Aquinas is not in this argument concerned with heat, cold, sweetness, sourness, fragrance, smelliness, and other mundane features of reality, Dawkins' objection simply misses the point. Moreover, it should now be clear why Aquinas takes the most true, most good, and most noble being to be one and the same being; for as we saw in chapter 2, Aquinas argues that the transcendentals are "convertible" with one another. That is to say, they are one and the same thing considered under different descriptions. This is also why he draws a related inference that might otherwise seem ungrounded to many modern readers, to the effect that that which is most true, good, and noble is "consequently, something which is uttermost being; for those things that are greatest in truth are greatest in being." For this follows automatically from the doctrine of the transcendentals.

We also saw in chapter 2 that Aquinas takes different aspects of reality all to have being in an analogical rather than univocal sense. Accidents and substances both have being, but a substance has independent existence in a way accidents do not; material things and angels both have being, but angels (since they lack matter and are composed of pure form together with an act of existence) are metaphysically simpler than material things and lack the tendency towards corruption that material things possess; created things and God both have being, but in created things essence and existence are distinct and in God they are not. Again, the way in which each has being is analogous to the way the others do, but not identical. In particular, it should be evident that substances have a higher degree of being than accidents do, angels a higher degree of being than material things do, and God a higher degree of being than any created thing; for substances lack the dependence on (other) substances that accidents have for their being, angels lack the dependence on matter that material things have for their being, and God depends on nothing at all for his existence but is rather that on which everything else depends. We see here a hierarchy in the order of being that dovetails with the hierarchy from prime matter through purely material things, human beings, and angels, up to God as Pure Act that we also had reason to discuss in chapter 2.

Given the convertibility of the transcendentals, it should not be surprising that, just as being does, goodness, truth, and the like come in degrees and are predicated of things analogically. For instance, the goodness or perfection of a triangle drawn carefully on paper with a pen and ruler is greater than that of a triangle drawn hastily in crayon on the cracked plastic seat of a moving bus, for it more perfectly instantiates the form or pattern definitive of triangularity. The goodness or perfection of someone who always tells the truth is greater than that of a habitual liar, for the former sort of person more perfectly fulfills the natural end or final cause of our intellectual and communicative faculties, which is to grasp and convey truth. A triangle and a person are both "good" in an analogical rather than a univocal sense, however, since there is a moral component to human goodness that is absent in the case of triangles and other non-rational entities. Moreover, human beings and triangles, along with other inanimate material things, plants, and non-human animals, manifest different degrees of goodness. Inanimate material things have certain perfections, such as (again) the straightness with which the sides of a triangle might be drawn. Plants, the simplest living things, have these sorts of perfections too given that they are material things, but in addition they have perfections that inanimate things do not have, namely the capacity to take in nutrients, grow, and reproduce themselves. Animals incorporate both the perfections of inanimate material things and plants, but in addition have the capacity for locomotion and sensation, which plants do not have. Human beings possess the perfections that inanimate material things, plants, and other animals have, but in addition have the capacity for intellect and will. Each of these levels of material being represents a higher level of goodness or perfection than the preceding one because it incorporates the perfections of the lower levels while adding perfections of its own. When we get to the purely immaterial levels of the hierarchy of being, we have entities which, though they lack the perfections of material things "formally," they nevertheless possess them "eminently" insofar as (unlike purely material things on Aquinas's view) they can grasp them intellectually (and grasp them intellectually in a way that is superior to our way of grasping them, since though the human intellect is immaterial, it is limited because of its dependence on sense organs).

We will have reason to explore some of these matters in more detail in our next chapter, but the point for now is to indicate the way in which Aquinas takes the degrees of goodness, being, and the like to point to a single maximum. The idea is that if we start by considering the natures of each of the lower levels of reality and then proceed to follow them upward, we find ourselves inexorably led to a highest level. In particular, degrees of goodness, truth, nobility, and so forth each point beyond themselves to a highest degree of each; since these are all convertible with one another, it is the *same* one maximum to which they all point; and since they are all in turn convertible with being, this single maximum is also that which is most fully real. What Aquinas is up to in the Fourth Way can therefore be understood when we read the argument in light of his doctrines of the transcendentals, analogy, and the hierarchy of being.

In what sense is this highest level of reality the "cause" of the lower levels? And in what sense do the latter "participate" in the former if it is not in a Platonic sense? The answers to these questions are related. Something "participates" in a certain perfection when it has that perfection only in a partial or limited way (*In DH* 2); and for Aquinas, "whatever is found in anything by participation, must be caused in it by that to which it belongs essentially" (*ST* I.44.1). Unlike Plato, whose emphasis is exclusively on what later thinkers would call formal causality, Aquinas takes there to be an essential link between participating in something and being *efficiently* caused by it. How so? Consider first the specific case of existence or being, where we have already seen that for Aquinas, "from the fact that a thing has being by participation, it follows that it is caused" (*ST* I.44.1). The reason for this was that if a thing's essence and existence are distinct (so that it only "participates" in being or existence rather than being identical with pure being or existence), only something outside the thing could give it existence or being; for to say that its existence derives from its essence (which is the only other alternative) would entail the absurdity that it causes itself. (Keep in mind that deriving or flowing from an essence is not the same as being identical with an essence; for example, the essence of a human being is to be a rational animal, and having the capacity for language flows or derives from this essence, but having the capacity for language is nevertheless not *identical* with being a rational animal.) We have also seen that, for Aquinas, the cause in question must ultimately be something in which its essence and existence are identical, and which accordingly just *is* being itself, or (we might now say) *unparticipated* being.

That, of course, is the heart of the "existential proof" and thus (I have suggested) the Second Way, which we have already examined. But given that being is convertible with goodness, truth, and the like, we would expect that what is true of things which have being or existence only by participation will also be true of things having goodness, truth, and so on only by participation, thus opening the way to a distinct argument for God's existence (namely the Fourth Way). And that is precisely what Aquinas thinks. In particular, he holds that in general (and not just with respect to being or existence) things that have some perfection only to various limited degrees must not have that perfection as part of their essence, "for if each one were of itself competent to have it, there would be no reason why one should have it more than another" (QDP 3.5). That is to say, if it were part of a thing's very *essence* to have the perfection, then there would be no reason for it not to possess it in an *unlimited* way. (Hence any human being is fully human, which follows from humanity being part of his or her essence, but does not have being to the fullest extent – which would be possible only for something whose essence just is being – or goodness to the fullest extent – which would be possible only for something in some sense having within it *every* perfection – and so forth.) So, for a limited thing to have some perfection, it must derive it from something outside it. And as Wippel notes, we would be led into a vicious infinite regress of the sort Aquinas has already criticized unless this something either is or is traceable to a cause which has the perfection to an unlimited degree.

But if the ultimate cause is unlimited in goodness, truth, nobility, or whatever other transcendental we are starting with, then (as we have already said) given the convertibility of the transcendentals it will also have to be unlimited in being and therefore just *be* pure being or existence itself. We are led therefore to the existence of the same being arrived at at the end of each of the first three ways – pure act, a being whose essence just is existence and which is the efficient cause of the being or actuality of everything other than itself – via yet another route, a consideration of the degrees of perfection found in the things of our experience.

The Fifth Way

The proof from finality starts with the observation that "things which lack intelligence, such as natural bodies, act for an end, and this is evident from their acting always, or nearly always, in the same way, so as to obtain the best result" (*ST* I.2.3). From this it is plain that they act "not fortuitously, but designedly" (*ST* I.2.3). But whatever lacks intelligence can only act for an end if it is directed by something which has intelligence, "as the arrow is shot to its mark by the archer" (*ST* I.2.3). "Therefore some intelligent being exists by whom all natural things are directed to their end; and this being we call God" (*ST* I.2.3).

Aquinas's first three Ways are all variations on what is known as the "cosmological argument" for the existence of God (from the Greek *kosmos* meaning "order"). The Fourth Way is sometimes called the "henological argument" (from the Greek *hen* or "one"). The Fifth Way, in turn, is commonly taken to be a version of the "teleological argument" (from the Greek *telos* meaning "end" or "goal"). Etymologically speaking, this is an apt name for the proof, but it is also potentially misleading given that when most contemporary philosophers hear the expression "teleological argument" they naturally think of the famous "design argument," associated historically with William Paley (1743–1805), and defended today by "Intelligent Design" theorists critical of Darwin's theory of evolution by natural selection. Indeed, many writers (such as Richard Dawkins) assume that the Fifth Way is just a variation on the "design argument." But in fact Aquinas's argument is radically different from Paley's, and the standard objections directed against the latter have no force against the former.

Paley's argument was roughly this. Like some human artifacts, the universe is extremely complex and orderly; and while it is theoretically possible that this complexity and order was the result of impersonal natural processes, it is far more likely that it is the work of an intelligent designer. Paley's favorite examples of complexity and order are living things and their various organs. His successors in the "Intelligent Design" movement, though they attempt to formulate their position with greater mathematical rigor than Paley did, have followed him in this emphasis, focusing as they do on the purported "irreducible complexity" of various biological structures. Critics of the design argument respond that this is "God of the gaps" reasoning of the sort that is constantly vulnerable to being overthrown by the latest scientific research, which may well reveal (as it has in the past) that what seems at first glance to be irreducibly complex can be accounted for in terms of more simple, and impersonal, natural processes.

Whatever side one takes in this debate, it is irrelevant to the evaluation of Aquinas's Fifth Way, which differs from the design argument of Paley and the "Intelligent Design" movement in several crucial respects. Paley's argument would justify, at most, belief in a deistic god who gave order to the world at some point in the past but who need not be appealed to in order to explain its current operation, which can be accounted for entirely in terms of impersonal laws of nature. "Intelligent Design" theorists even acknowledge that their arguments do not necessarily imply a deity at all, but merely a superhuman intelligence of some sort or other. Aquinas, by contrast, takes the Fifth Way to entail the existence of nothing less than the God of classical theism, who sustains the order of the world *here and now* and at any moment at which it exists. Moreover, while Paley and his contemporary successors claim only that the existence of a designer is *probable*, Aquinas takes the Fifth Way *conclusively to establish* the truth of its conclusion. Related to this, whereas the design argument is typically presented as a kind of quasi-scientific empirical hypothesis, Aquinas's argument is intended as a metaphysical demonstration. His claim is not that the existence of God is *one* possible explanation among others (albeit the best)

of the order that exists in the universe (which is how "God of
the gaps" arguments proceed) but rather that it can be seen on
analysis to be the *only* possible explanation *even in principle*. While
Paley and his successors focus on complex biological structures,
Aquinas is not especially interested either in biology or
complexity per se; even extremely simple inorganic phenomena
suffice in his view to show that a Supreme Intelligence exists.
Hence, while Darwin's theory of evolution by natural selection
is notoriously problematic for the design argument, it is totally
irrelevant to the Fifth Way. (That is not to say that Aquinas
would agree that *every* aspect of the biological realm can be
explained in the materialistic terms favored by Darwinians; as we
will see in the next chapter, he would definitely not agree with
this. The point is just that the debate over evolution is not
relevant to the *Fifth Way* specifically.) And all of these dissimi-
larities derive ultimately from one key difference between the
design argument and the Fifth Way, which is that whereas the
former takes for granted a "mechanical" conception of the
natural world of the sort early modern philosophers and scientists sought to put in place of Aristotelian teleology, Aquinas's
argument crucially presupposes that final causes are as real and
objective a feature of the natural world as gravity or electromagnetism.

We saw in chapter 2 how the reality of final causes might be
defended today. We also saw that the sense in which teleology
pervades the natural world on Aquinas's view is that efficient
causes would not be intelligible without final causes. This is
what he means when he says in the Fifth Way that "things
which lack intelligence, such as natural bodies, act for an end,
and this is evident from their acting always, or nearly always, in
the same way, so as to obtain the best result." He is not
especially interested here in the fact that hearts typically pump
blood, that eyes enable us to see, and other such biological facts
(though these would naturally be included as instances of the

more general phenomenon he is interested in). It is the existence of *any causal regularities at all* that he takes to require explanation (where the emphasis here, unlike in the Second Way, is on the "regularities" part of this phrase rather than the "causal" part). For Aquinas, the fact that A regularly brings about B, as B's *efficient* cause, entails that bringing about B is in turn the *final* cause of A. For if we did not suppose that A inherently "points to" or is "directed towards" the generation of B as its natural end, then we would have no way to account for the fact that A typically does generate *B* specifically, rather than C, or D, or E, or indeed rather than no effect at all. Of course, some interfering factor might prevent A from bringing about its typical effect, or from bringing it about fully or perfectly; this is why Aquinas speaks of a cause bringing about the "best" or perfect result at least "*nearly* always." But these unusual cases can only be understood against the background of the typical case, and in particular in light of the fact that a cause inherently *points to* the best or most perfect realization of its effect, even if it might sometimes be prevented by circumstances from bringing it about.

When Aquinas says that natural bodies do not bring about their effects "fortuitously," then, he is not arguing (as advocates of the design argument might) that it is improbable that complex structures could arise by chance, which would invite the response that natural selection shows how such structures might nevertheless arise by non-fortuitous but impersonal processes. For, to repeat, he is not interested here in complexity per se in the first place; as Garrigou-Lagrange points out, even a simple physical phenomenon like the attraction between two particles would suffice for his purposes. What he is saying is rather that it is impossible that *every* apparent causal regularity can be attributed to chance, for chance itself presupposes causal regularity. To take a stock example, for Aquinas, a paradigmatically fortuitous event would be a farmer's discovery of treasure under the ground he is plowing. Such a discovery was not in any sense intended – neither by the farmer nor by the person who buried the treasure, and not by nature either insofar as there is no causal law entailing that treasure will tend to be uncovered when one plows the ground. All the same, the farmer did intend to plow the ground, someone did intend to bury the treasure, and there are all sorts of causal laws operative when the farmer happens fortuitously to uncover treasure. Hence chance presupposes a background of causal factors which themselves neither have anything to do with chance nor can plausibly be accounted for without reference to final causality, so that it would be incoherent to suppose that an appeal to chance might somehow eliminate the need to appeal to final causality.

Given what Aquinas says about chance (and as Garrigou-Lagrange has also pointed out), it is a mistake to think that the "principle of finality" on which Aquinas's argument rests says that "*everything* has a final cause" (just as, as we have seen, it is a mistake to assume that the principle of causality says that "everything has an efficient cause"). For not "everything" does have a final cause, given the existence of chance events. What Aquinas actually says, as we have seen, is that every *agent* has a final cause; that is to say, that everything that serves as an efficient cause "points to" or is "directed at" some specific effect or range of effects as its natural end. This is why it is silly to ask (as is sometimes done) "What is the purpose of a mountain range?" or "What is the purpose of an asteroid?" as if such questions must be an embarrassment to any Aristotelian. Aquinas would be happy to allow that such things might turn out to serve no "purpose," in the sense of being accidental byproducts of convergent natural processes (plate tectonics or volcanism in the former case, say, and collisions between larger celestial bodies in the latter). He would insist, however, and quite plausibly, that such natural processes embody patterns of efficient causation that are themselves intelligible only in terms of final causation. And precisely for that reason, to the extent that biological processes like evolution manifest causal regularities, they if anything only *support* the Fifth Way rather than undermine it. For as with mountains, asteroids, and the like, even if it should turn out that animal species are the accidental byproducts of various convergent impersonal causal processes, the existence of those evolutionary processes themselves would require explanation in terms of final causes.

As these considerations together with those examined in chapter 2 indicate, then, the reality of final causes, in both the inorganic and organic realms, is as defensible today as it ever was. But if there really are final causes, then the first part of Aquinas's Fifth Way is vindicated. But what of the second stage of the argument, which claims that unintelligent natural processes can only act for an end if directed by some intelligence? The first thing to say is that this is not, as it might at first seem, a mere variation on the sort of reasoning represented by Paley's design argument. Paley, taking for granted as he does a modern mechanistic view of nature, denies that purpose or teleology is *immanent* or *inherent* to the natural order. That is why his argument is a merely probabilistic one. The design argument allows that there *might* in fact be no purpose at all in the natural world, but only the misleading appearance of purpose; its claim is simply that, at least where complex mechanistic processes are concerned, this supposition is unlikely. And even if there is purpose, it is imposed from outside, in just the way a human watchmaker imposes a certain order on metal parts that have no *inherent* tendency to function as a timepiece. The natural world remains as devoid of immanent teleology after the designer's action as before. Moreover, as with a watch, once Paley's designer has done his "watchmaking," there is no need for him to remain on the scene, for once built the mechanism can function without him.

There is nothing like this kind of reasoning going on in Aquinas's Fifth Way. Like Aristotle, Aquinas takes the teleology or final causality that exists in nature to be immanent to it, to such an extent that one could for practical purposes (and as Aristotle himself did) ignore the idea of a designer altogether when searching out the final causes of things in the course of doing physical and biological science. (Note how different this is from the approach of contemporary "Intelligent Design" theorists.) A struck match generates fire and heat rather than frost and cold; an acorn always grows into an oak rather than a rosebush or a dog; the moon goes around the earth in a smooth elliptical orbit rather than zigzagging erratically; the heart pumps blood continuously and doesn't stop and start several times a day; condensation results in precipitation which results in collection which results in evaporation which in turn results in condensation; and so forth. In each of these cases and in countless others we have regularities that point to ends or goals, usually totally unconscious, which are just built into nature and can be known through observation to be there whether or not it ever occurs to anyone to ask how they got there. In particular, one can know that there are these ends, goals, or purposes in nature whether or not it ever occurs to anyone to consider the purposes, or even the existence, of a *designer* of nature.

Still, even if (as Aristotle and Aquinas would hold) the existence of such final causes is obvious and unavoidable, it is very odd that there should be such things, and their existence requires explanation even though that explanation, whatever it is, is not something we need worry about for the purposes of everyday scientific research. One of the common objections to the very idea of final causation is that it seems to entail that a thing can produce an effect even before that thing exists. Hence to say that an oak tree is the final cause of an acorn seems to entail that the oak tree – which doesn't exist yet – in some sense causes the acorn to pass through every stage it must reach on the way to becoming an oak, since the oak is the "goal" or natural end of the acorn. But how can this be?

Consider those cases where goal-directedness is associated with consciousness, as it is in us. A builder builds a house, and he is able to do so because the effect, the house, exists as an idea in his intellect before it exists in reality. That is the way in which the house serves as the *final* cause of the actions of the builder even as those actions are the *efficient* cause of the house. Indeed, that is the *only* way the house can do so. For a cause, to have any efficacy, must in some sense exist; and if it doesn't exist in reality, then the only place left for it to exist (certainly for Aquinas, who as an Aristotelian does not accept Plato's notion of a "third realm" beyond the natural world and the mind) is in the intellect.

What then of the vast system of causes that constitutes the physical universe? Every one of them is directed towards a certain end or final cause. Yet almost none of them is associated with any thought, consciousness, or intellect at all; and even animals and human beings, which are conscious, are comprised in whole or in part of unconscious and unintelligent material components which themselves manifest final causality. But given what was said above, it is impossible for anything to be directed towards an end unless that end exists in an intellect which directs the thing in question towards it. It follows that the system of ends or final causes that make up the physical universe can only exist at all if there is a Supreme Intelligence or intellect outside the universe which directs things towards their ends. Moreover, this intellect must exist *here and now*, and not merely at some beginning point in the past, because causes are *here and now*, and at any point at which they exist at all, directed towards certain ends (otherwise, for reasons examined already, they wouldn't on Aquinas's analysis be true efficient causes at all). As with Aquinas's other arguments, he is not concerned here with whether and how the universe might have begun, but rather with what keeps it as it is at any given moment, a question which must arise even if the universe had no beginning. Hence the Supreme Intelligence of the Fifth Way is not the deistic god that seems to be the most Paley can argue for. Moreover, given his metaphysical assumptions, Aquinas's conclusion follows necessarily and not merely with probability. In these respects (and not only in these respects, as we shall see) the Fifth Way reaches a much stronger conclusion than the design argument, and does so precisely because unlike the design argument it starts from the recognition of the existence of immanent teleology.

Now we saw in chapter 2 that Aquinas regards the final cause as the "cause of causes" insofar as it determines the other causes. In particular, for a thing to have a certain final cause entails that it also has a certain formal and material cause and thus a certain nature or essence; otherwise its final cause would not be inherent in it, nor would it be capable of realizing it. For "upon the form follows an inclination to the end … for everything, in so far as it is in act, acts and tends towards that which is in accordance with its form" (*ST* I.5.5; cf. *QDV* 25.1). But we have also seen that on Aquinas's view, for a contingent thing to be real, its essence must be conjoined to an act of existence, that this can only be accomplished by something outside it, and that the ultimate cause of its existence must be something in which essence and existence are identical. It follows that whatever orders things to their ends must also be the cause of those things and thus (given what was said earlier) Pure Act or Being Itself. Furthermore, as Garrigou-Lagrange points out, if the Supreme Intelligence were not Pure Act or Being Itself, then its essence would be distinct from its existence, and thus it would have a potency or potential (for existence) which, like all potencies, is of its nature directed towards an end. But in that case there would have to be a higher intelligence directing that potency to its end, and we would be off on exactly the sort of regress that, for reasons we have already seen, must in Aquinas's view terminate in a first member. To explain the reality of final causes, then, we are, once again, unavoidably led to a Supreme Intelligence which is also Pure Act or Being Itself.

Obviously all of this goes beyond what Aquinas says in the text of the Fifth Way itself, which, like the other ways, is intended only as a summary. The point is that, when fully worked out in light of Aquinas's more general metaphysical commitments, the Fifth Way can be seen to lead to precisely the same sort of being whose existence is argued for in the other four ways, by yet another route. And since this being would (if Aquinas's more general metaphysical assumptions are correct) have to be Pure Act or Being Itself, we can see yet again that, if it succeeds, the Fifth Way establishes far more than the finite sort of being reached via the arguments of Paley and his successors in the "Intelligent Design" movement.

Though its approach is very different from Paley's, it might still seem as if the Fifth Way conflicts with Aristotle's view that final causality can exist even in the absence of consciousness. But that there is no conflict here can perhaps be seen by considering the analogy of language. If we consider the words and sentences we speak and write, it is obvious that they get their meaning from the community of language users that produces them, and ultimately from the ideas expressed by those language users in using them. Apart from these users, these linguistic items would be nothing more than meaningless noises or splotches of ink. Still, once produced, they take on a kind of life of their own. Words, sentences, and the like printed in books or recorded on tape retain their meaning even when no one is thinking about them; indeed, even if the books or tapes in question sit in a dusty corner of a library or archive somewhere, ignored for decades and completely forgotten, they still retain their meaning for all that. Moreover, language has a structure that most language users are unaware of, but which can be studied by linguists. And so forth. Still, if the community of language users were to disappear entirely – every single one of them killed in a worldwide plague, say – then the recorded words that were left behind *would* in that case revert to meaningless sounds or marks. While the community of language users exists, its general background presence is all that is required for meaning to persist in the physical sounds and markings, even if some of those sounds and markings are not the subject of anyone's attention at a particular moment. But if the community goes away altogether, the meaning goes with it. By analogy (and it is only an analogy, and admittedly not an exact one) we might think of the relationship of the Supreme Intelligence of the Fifth Way to the system of final causes in the world as somewhat like the relationship of language users to language. The Supreme Intelligence directs things to their ends, but the system thereby created has a kind of independence insofar as it can be studied without reference to the Supreme Intelligence himself, just as linguists can study the structure of language without paying attention to the intentions of this or that language user. The ends are in a sense just "there" in unconscious causes like the meaning is just "there" in words once they have been written. At the same time, if the Supreme Intelligence were to cease directing things towards their ends, final causes would immediately disappear, just as the meaning of words would disappear if all language users disappeared.

The divine attributes

As we have said, at least when the proofs are read in light of Aquinas's general metaphysical commitments, each of the Five Ways can be seen, if successful, to demonstrate the existence of a being who is Pure Act or Being Itself. Does this mean that they all converge on *one and the same* being, or might the existence of five distinct "gods" be proved via Aquinas's arguments? Aquinas's answer should be clear from what was said in chapter 2 about his doctrine of essence and existence. For the reasons we examined then, on Aquinas's view there can in principle be only one being whose essence and existence are identical, and thus which is Pure Being. Hence it is necessarily one and the same being on which all five proofs converge. This would obviously entail, for the same reason, that there is and can be only one God. For there to be more than one God, there would have to be some essence that the distinct "Gods" all share, each with his own individual act of existence. But since God is that being in whom essence and existence are identical, who just *is* existence or being itself, there is no sense to be made of the idea that he shares an essence with anything else, or has one act of existing alongside others (*ST* I.11.3).

Aquinas also gives two other reasons for holding that the being whose existence is argued for in the Five Ways is necessarily unique. For there to be more than one such being, there would have to be some way to distinguish one from another, and this could only be in terms of some perfection or privation that one has but the other lacks. But as Pure Act, such a being would be devoid of all imperfections and privations, since imperfections and privations are just different ways in which something could fail to be in act or actual. Hence there can be no way even in principle to distinguish one such being from another, and thus there could not possibly be more than one (*ST* I.11.3). Furthermore, the order that characterizes the world gives it a unity that is explicable only if there is also unity in its cause (*ST* I.11.3).

The *unity* or oneness of God is only one of many divine attributes that Aquinas thinks can be established via pure reason without recourse to divine revelation. We have space here only to provide a brief survey, but Aquinas himself pursues the matter at great length and by deploying a wealth of arguments both in the *Summa Theologiae* and elsewhere, thus exposing as a kind of urban legend the commonly made allegation that even if one were to accept the existence of a first cause, unmoved mover, and so on, Aquinas does nothing to show that such a being would have the other characteristics traditionally ascribed to God. The Five Ways are meant by themselves only to establish the existence of a being having certain key attributes, such as being an unmoved mover, Pure Act, Being Itself, and so forth. Aquinas's next move is to argue that anything having these key features can be seen on analysis necessarily to possess also the other attributes commonly ascribed to God. He follows Pseudo-Dionysius in taking a threefold approach to knowledge of God's attributes (*ST* I.13.8): the way of causality (*via causalitatis*), whereby we move from knowledge of the world to knowledge of God as cause of the world; the way of negation (*via negativa*), whereby we deny of God any characteristic incompatible with his being the first cause and thus Pure Act; and the way of eminence (*via eminentia*), whereby we conclude, by applying the principle of proportionate causality described in chapter 2, that God can be said to possess in an eminent way certain features we attribute to things in the world. As this indicates, while it is sometimes claimed that Aquinas agreed with thinkers like Moses Maimonides that our knowledge of God is purely negative, knowledge of what God is not rather than what he is, this was not in fact his view; indeed, he explicitly repudiates it (*ST* I.13.2). The *via negativa* obviously gives us only negative knowledge of God, but the *via causalitatis* and the *via eminentia* give us some positive knowledge too.

Several attributes seem to follow immediately and obviously from God's being Pure Act. Since to change is to be reduced from potency to act, that which is Pure Act, devoid of all potency, must be *immutable* or incapable of change (*ST* I.9.1). Since material things are of their nature compounds of act and potency, that which is Pure Act must be *immaterial* and thus *incorporeal* or without any sort of body (*ST* I.3.1–2). Since such a being is immutable and time (as Aquinas argues) cannot exist apart from change, that which is Pure Act must also be *eternal*, outside time altogether, without beginning or end (*ST* I.10.1–2).

As the cause of the world, God obviously has *power*, for "all operation proceeds from power" (*QDP* 1.1; cf. *ST* I.25.1). Moreover, "the more actual a thing is the more it abounds in active power," so that as Pure Act, God must be infinite in power (*QDP* 1.2; cf. *ST* I.25.2). In line with the mainstream classical theistic tradition, Aquinas holds that since there is no sense to be made of doing what is intrinsically impossible (e.g. making a round square or something else involving a self-contradiction), to say that God is omnipotent does not entail that he can do such things, but only that he can do whatever is intrinsically possible (*ST* I.25.3).

The Fifth Way, if successful, establishes by itself that God has *intellect*. Furthermore, intelligent beings are distinguished from non-intelligent ones in that the latter, but not the former, possess only their own forms. For an "intelligent being is naturally adapted to have also the form of some other thing; for the idea of the thing known is in the knower" (*ST* I.14.1). That is to say, to understand some thing is for that thing's essence to exist in some sense in one's own intellect. Now the reason non-intelligent things lack this ability to have the form of another thing is that they are wholly material, and material things can only possess one form at a time, as it were. Hence immaterial beings can possess the forms of other things precisely because they are immaterial; and the further a thing is from materiality, the more powerful its intellect is bound to be. Thus human beings, which, though they have immaterial intellects are also embodied, are less intelligent than angels, which are incorporeal. "Since therefore God is in the highest degree of immateriality ... it follows that He occupies the highest place in knowledge" (*ST* I.14.1). This argument presupposes a number of theses in the philosophy of mind and cannot be evaluated, or even properly understood, unless those theses are first understood. We will explore these theses in chapter 4.

We can also conclude, in Aquinas's view, that "there is will in God, as there is intellect: since will follows upon intellect"

(*ST* I.19.1). Why do will and intellect necessarily go together? For Aquinas, things naturally are inclined or tend towards their natural forms, and will not of themselves rest, as it were, until that form is perfectly realized; hence the acorn, for example, has a built-in tendency towards realizing the form of an oak, and will naturally realize that form unless somehow prevented by something outside it. What we are describing in this example is of course the goal-directedness of the acorn as something having a final cause. But other sorts of thing have final causes too. In sentient beings, namely animals, this inclination towards the perfection of their forms is what we call appetite. And in beings with intellect it is what we call will. Thus anything having an intellect must have will. (We will return to this topic in the next chapter.) Of course, since God does not have the limitations we have, he does not have any ends he needs to fulfill, any more than he needs to acquire any knowledge. Thus, as with our attribution of power, intellect, and other attributes to God, our attribution of will to him is intended in an *analogous* rather than a univocal sense.

Since something is perfect to the degree it is in act or actual, God as Pure Act must be *perfect* (*ST* I.4.1). Given the convertibility of being and goodness, God as Pure Act and Being Itself must also be *good*, indeed the highest good (*ST* I.6). At this point, it might be objected that the problem of evil casts doubt on this claim; for if God is good, why hasn't he eliminated the evil that obviously exists in the world? But there are several problems with this objection. First of all, it could only undermine Aquinas's argument for God's goodness if we assumed that a good being could not possibly have a reason to allow evil. But it is notoriously difficult to show that such a being *could not possibly* have such a reason, and even most contemporary atheist philosophers would not make such a strong claim. In the absence of such an assumption, though, Aquinas could simply insist that since his arguments have proven that God exists and is good, it follows that whatever evil exists must be consistent with his goodness.

Second, as Aquinas himself argues in reply to the problem of evil, "this is part of the infinite goodness of God, that He should allow evil to exist, and out of it produce good" (*ST* I.2.3). That is to say, the reason God allows evil is precisely because he intends to bring good out of it, whether that good is that we come to learn from the mistakes we make, that we come to have certain virtues that could not be acquired without struggling against evil, that we come to appreciate what is good by contrast with what is evil, or whatever. And given that God is omnipotent and that (as we shall see in the next chapter) Aquinas holds that we have immortal souls, so that our time on earth is merely a brief prelude to an everlasting existence in the hereafter, it is hardly implausible to suggest that God is capable of rewarding us with a good in the next life that is so tremendous that even the most horrendous evils in this life will come to seem trivial in comparison, and worth having suffered through. Of course, in the face of the worst real-world evils, the idea of such a good in the hereafter can seem cold, abstract, and remote. But that is an emotional problem rather than an intellectual one; it has no tendency to show that there is or could be no such good, but only that it is hard for us to keep our minds fixed on it in the face of suffering. Nor could an atheist dismiss such a response out of hand without begging the question. To say "There is no God, because of all the unredeemable evil that exists; and the evil that exists must be unredeemable, because there is no God who could redeem it," would be to argue in a circle.

Third, as Brian Davies has emphasized, much discussion of the problem of evil seems to presuppose that God is a kind of moral agent who has certain duties which (so it is alleged) he has failed to live up to. But this way of thinking simply makes no sense given Aquinas's conception of God. For only creatures with the sorts of limitations we have can coherently be described as having moral duties. For example, given that we depend on other people for our well-being and they depend on us, we have certain obligations towards each other; given that we have certain potentials the realization of which is good for us, potentials which require a certain amount of effort to realize, we have a duty to make that effort; and so forth. But as Pure Act and Being Itself, God has none of these dependencies, potentials, or limitations, and thus there is no sense to be made of the suggestion that he either has or lacks this or that moral virtue or has lived up to or failed to live up to this or that moral obligation. Though his possession of intellect and will (or, more precisely, of something analogous to what we call intellect and will in us) entails that he is in some sense "personal" (rather than the sort of impersonal deity familiar from certain Eastern religions), God is nevertheless not "a person" in the sense that we are, with all the limitations that expression implies.

That God is very remote indeed from the things of our experience is nowhere clearer than in Aquinas's account of divine *simplicity*, which is perhaps the most controversial aspect of his teaching on the divine attributes. For Aquinas, God is "simple" in the sense of being in no way composed of parts (*ST* I.3). As has been said, he is incorporeal and immaterial, and thus cannot have any bodily parts nor be composed of form and matter. But neither does he have even any metaphysical parts. For as we have also seen, on Aquinas's account there is no distinction between essence and existence in God. Unlike everything else that exists, he just *is* his own existence, and just *is* his own essence, for these are identical. For this reason, there can also be no distinction between genus and difference in God, since *being*, the only candidate genus for something whose essence and existence are identical is (as we saw in chapter 2) no genus at all, and since for there to be a member of a genus, it must have an act of existence which differs from the essence it shares (at least potentially) with other members of the genus, and, again, there is no distinction between essence and existence in God. Hence, again, "it is clear that God is nowise composite, but is altogether simple" (*ST* I.3.7).

One famous implication of this doctrine is that though we distinguish in thought between God's eternity, power, goodness, intellect, will, and so forth, in God himself there is no distinction between any of the divine attributes. God's eternity *is* his power, which *is* his goodness, which *is* his intellect, which *is* his will, and so on. Indeed, *God himself* just is his power, his goodness, and so on, just as he just *is* his existence, and just *is* his essence. Talking or conceiving of God, God's essence, God's existence, God's power, God's goodness, and so forth are really all just different ways of talking or conceiving of one and the very same thing. Though we distinguish between them in thought, there is no distinction at all between them in reality. For, again, if there were such a distinction, then we could distinguish parts in God, and being absolutely simple, God has no parts.

Though the idea of divine simplicity might seem odd or eccentric to some contemporary readers, it is historically speaking the mainstream view of God's nature within the classical theistic tradition, being defended not only by Aquinas, but by thinkers as diverse as St. Athanasius, St. Augustine, St. Anselm, Maimonides, Avicenna, and Averroes, to name just a few. It is affirmed in such councils of the Roman Catholic Church as the Fourth Lateran Council (1215) and Vatican I (1869–1870). Nevertheless, it has been criticized by a number of contemporary philosophers and theologians. Some of this criticism derives from objections to Aquinas's doctrine of the identity of essence and existence in God, which were discussed in chapter 2. Some of it derives from worries over whether it makes sense to say that God's power is identical to his goodness, which is identical to his intellect, and so on; for wouldn't this entail that power is the same thing as goodness, goodness the same thing as intellect, and so forth, which is obviously false? But this does not in fact follow. For one thing, just as (to use Frege's famous example) we can acknowledge that the expressions "the morning star" and "the evening star" differ in *sense* while consistently affirming that they *refer* to one and the same thing (the planet Venus), so too can we acknowledge the obvious fact that "power," "goodness," "intellect," and so on differ in sense while insisting that when applied to God they refer to one and the same thing. For another thing, we must keep in mind Aquinas's doctrine of analogy, according to which, while the terms we apply to created things do not apply to God in either equivocal or univocal senses, they do apply in analogical senses. So, while it would of course be absurd to say that power, goodness, intellect, and so forth are all identical in God if we were using these terms in exactly the same sense in which we apply them to ourselves, it is not absurd to say that there is in God something that is *analogous* to power, something *analogous* to goodness, something *analogous* to intellect, and so on, and that these "somethings" all turn out to be one and the same thing.

As Eleonore Stump has noted, there are also in any case certain advantages of the doctrine of divine simplicity that ought to recommend it at least to philosophers otherwise sympathetic with Aquinas's attempt to prove the existence of God via cosmological arguments and/or with the idea that there is an important link between the existence of God and the foundations of morality. To take the latter issue first, there is a distinction commonly drawn between the view that something counts as good or bad because of God's will and the view that God wills for us to do or to avoid doing something because it is either good or bad by reference to some standard external to him, and neither of these views is theologically satisfactory. The first seems to make morality entirely arbitrary, insofar as it appears to entail for example that torturing infants for fun would have been good if God had willed this. The second seems to entail that morality is ultimately independent of God, which seems incompatible with the idea that everything that exists other than God ultimately derives from him. This is the basis for the "Euthyphro dilemma" (named after a dialogue of Plato's in which it was famously put forward), which is an attempt to refute the thesis that morality depends on God by arguing that there are only these two ways of understanding this thesis and that neither of them can be acceptable to the theist. But as Stump points out, the doctrine of divine simplicity shows that there is a third option here, so that the dilemma in question is a false one. For if God just *is* perfect goodness which just *is* the divine will which just *is* immutable and necessary being, then there can be no question either of God willing in accordance with some standard of goodness independent of him or of his will being arbitrary. What is objectively good and what God wills for us as morally obligatory are just *the same thing* considered under different descriptions, and neither could have been other than they are. (We will return to this issue when we examine Aquinas's moral theory in chapter 5.)

Stump notes also that the doctrine of divine simplicity affords certain advantages to versions of the cosmological argument informed by it. For example, as we noted earlier, some modern versions of the cosmological argument hold that only God can serve as the ultimate explanation of why the universe exists because he is a being whose essence "includes" existence, as if existence were one "property" of God alongside and distinct from other ones, a property which is also distinct from the essence which "includes" it and from the divine being who "possesses" it. The trouble with this is that it seems perfectly possible to detach "existence" so conceived from God's other "properties"; certainly the assertion that existence must necessarily go together with them seems arbitrary and itself in need of explanation. But if God just *is* his existence which just *is* his power, which just *is* his will, and so on, then this problem disappears.

Much more could be said about Aquinas's account of the divine attributes, but this much suffices to show that there is no basis whatsoever for the widespread assumption that Aquinas never justifies the claim that the being whose existence he argues for in the Five Ways is the God of traditional theism. It also gives a sense of how much Aquinas thinks we can know about God through purely philosophical reasoning. But there is also a sense in which Aquinas thinks that we ultimately cannot know the *essence* of God, at least not as it is in itself. For in the strict sense knowledge of the essence of a thing requires the ability to define it in terms of its genus and difference, and as we have seen, there is for Aquinas no distinction in God between genus and difference, and thus no way to define him (*CT* 26). It is in *this* sense that Aquinas holds that "we cannot know what God is, but rather what He is not" (*ST* I.3). And this is why the famous ontological argument associated with St. Anselm is not considered by Aquinas to be one of the ways in which we might prove the existence of God. For Anselm, God is by definition the greatest conceivable being, and it is (Anselm holds) greater to exist than not to exist. Hence if God did not exist it would follow, absurdly, that there could be something conceivably greater than the greatest being. Anselm's argument thus begins with a definition of God's essence and attempts to show that given knowledge of that essence, we can know also that there must be something in reality corresponding to it, and thus that God exists. Since Aquinas holds that God's essence and existence are identical, he agrees that if we could have knowledge of God's essence we could see that he must exist. But since in fact we cannot, in his view, have knowledge of that essence, we cannot know the starting point of the ontological argument (*ST* I.2.1). Our knowledge of God must therefore be *a posteriori*, based on observation of his effects. But that, as we have seen, affords us in Aquinas's view with ample grounds indeed for affirming God's existence and predicating of him the traditional divine attributes.

4
Psychology

As I have emphasized throughout this book, understanding Aquinas requires "thinking outside the box" of the basic metaphysical assumptions (concerning cause, effect, substance, essence, etc.) that contemporary philosophers tend to take for granted. This is nowhere more true than where Aquinas's philosophy of mind is concerned. Indeed, to speak of Aquinas's "philosophy of mind" is already misleading. For Aquinas does not approach the issues dealt with in this modern philosophical sub-discipline in terms of their relevance to solving the so-called "mind–body problem." No such problem existed in Aquinas's day, and for him the important distinction was in any case not between mind and body, but rather between soul and body. Even that is potentially misleading, however, for Aquinas does not mean by "soul" what contemporary philosophers tend to mean by it, that is, an immaterial substance of the sort affirmed by Descartes. Furthermore, while contemporary philosophers of mind tend to obsess over the questions of whether and how science can explain consciousness and the "qualia" that define it, Aquinas instead takes what is now called "intentionality" to be the distinctive feature of the mind, and the one that it is in principle impossible to explain in materialistic terms. At the same time, he does not think of intentionality in quite the way contemporary philosophers do. Moreover, while he is not a materialist, he is not a Cartesian dualist either, his view being in some respects a middle position between these options. But neither is this middle position the standard one discussed by contemporary philosophers under the label "property dualism." And so forth.

To the modern philosophical reader, all this might make Aquinas sound very odd indeed, confusing and perhaps confused. (Readers unacquainted with contemporary philosophy of mind might find some of the terminology just used itself confusing; all will be explained presently.) Yet had Aquinas been familiar with the ideas of contemporary philosophers of mind, he would have regarded them as the confused ones, and in particular as having gotten the basic conceptual lay of the land totally wrong. For the "mind–body problem" is essentially an artifact of the early modern philosophers' decision to abandon a hylemorphic conception of the world for a mechanistic one, and its notorious intractability is, in the view of Thomists, one of the starkest indications of how deeply mistaken that decision was.

The soul

But we will come back to all that. Let us begin at the beginning, with Aquinas's conception of human nature in general. Here as elsewhere, Aquinas's position is built on an Aristotelian foundation. Recall that for Aristotle, the objects of our experience are composites of form and matter. Neither the form alone is the substance nor the matter alone, but both together, the form constituting the "act" or actuality of the substance and the matter its "potencies" or potentials. This is the doctrine of hylemorphism, and it applies to living things as well as to inanimate objects. Indeed, the distinction between soul and body is just a special case of the distinction between form and matter, which is itself a special case of the distinction between act and potency. That is to say, "the soul is the form of the body" (*In DA* II.1.234), the specific kind of form which makes the body a living thing as opposed to an inanimate object, which makes it actual in just the unique ways living things are. Since the soul is just that which makes the difference between living and non-living things, it can also be defined as "the first principle of life in those things which live" (*ST* I.75.1). "Soul" translates the Latin *anima*, which is why living things are sometimes said to be "animated." It also translates the Greek *psuche*, which is where the term "psychology" comes from. Psychology, for Aristotle and Aquinas, is not merely the study of the mind, but the study of that which makes the organism as a whole a living thing, and of the mind only insofar as it is an aspect of the whole organism.

Now it is crucial, if one is to avoid misunderstanding Aquinas's position here, that one put out of one's mind the popular conception of the soul, and even the standard modern philosophical conception. Viewers of the movie *Ghost* might think that what Aquinas has in mind is the sort of thing that floated out of the Patrick Swayze character's body after his death, an intangible but occasionally visible something which has the same size, shape, and general appearance as the living person. Readers of Descartes might assume that what he has in mind is the idea of an immaterial substance, a complete object existing in its own right which simply happens not to be a physical object. It might then be concluded that when Aristotle and Aquinas say that a soul is what makes something a living thing, what they mean is that a thing is alive only when it is being possessed by a ghost, or only when an immaterial substance is interacting with it. And it might then in turn be concluded that they are indulging in the rankest superstition, or at best appealing to a now scientifically discredited doctrine of "vitalism" (a term of abuse that is flung around more frequently than it is actually defined, but which in the minds of those who do the flinging seems to connote something like the belief in a kind of non-physical or quasi-physical stuff which when added to matter gives rise to life).

In fact the position of Aristotle and Aquinas has nothing to do with any of this. For them the soul is neither a ghost, nor an immaterial substance, nor some spooky kind of "stuff," non-physical, quasi-physical or otherwise. Nor are they present-ing a pseudo-scientific empirical hypothesis on which the existence of the soul is "postulated" as the best way of "explain-ing" how matter can have the form of a living thing. Again, by "soul" they just *mean* the form of a living thing, so that anything with such a form has a soul by definition. Attributing souls to living things is thus no more mysterious than saying that rubber balls and rocks each have forms that set them apart from other kinds of thing. Neither is it any more informative than that, and it is not meant to be. "Soul" simply names one kind of form among others.

At least given the general framework of hylemorphism, then, it is not the existence of the soul that is particularly problematic, but rather its nature. What *is* it exactly to have the form of a living thing? Or in other words, what sets living things apart from non-living ones? From the Aristotelian point of view, the answer is that "life is essentially that by which anything has power to move itself" (*In DA* II.1.219). Of course, we saw in earlier chapters that in Aquinas's view nothing can move or change itself in the strict sense; even the self-movement of an animal ultimately involves one part being moved by another. So talk of that which can "move itself" is meant here only in a loose sense. In particular, what Aquinas has in mind is evident from his statement elsewhere in the same passage to the effect that "we call those things inanimate which are moved only from outside." Similarly, he says that "the word *life* is used of all things which have in them the principle of their own activity" (*QDV* 4.8) and that "all things are said to be alive that determine themselves to movement or operation of any kind" (*ST* I.18.1). A living thing is just the sort of thing whose activities spring from *within*. When a dog races down a hill chasing a cat, its movement is of a different sort than that of a rock which rolls down a hill as a result of an earthquake; there is something *inter-nal* to the dog that causes its movement in a way there is nothing internal to the rock that causes its movement. This is so even though the dog's motion involves one internal part moving another, and even though it is ultimately God, as the first unmoved mover, who is responsible for the motion of both the rock and the dog.

To use some traditional Scholastic jargon, the key to the difference between living and non-living things lies in the distinction between *immanent* and *transeunt* (or "transient") causation. Immanent causation begins and remains within the agent or cause (though it may also and at the same time have some external effects); and typically it in some way involves the fulfillment or perfection of the cause. Transeunt causation, by contrast, is directed entirely outwardly, from the cause to an external effect. An animal's digestion of a meal would be an example of immanent causation, since the process begins and remains within the animal and serves to fulfill or perfect it by allowing it to stay alive and grow. One rock knocking another one off the side of a cliff would be an example of transeunt causation. Living things can serve as transeunt causes, but what is characteristic of them is that they are also capable of immanent causation in a way that non-living things are not. A living thing can undertake activity that is *perfective* of it, that *fulfills* it or *furthers its own good*, while non-living things cannot do this. In this way it aims at a unique kind of end or goal, though it is only its having this specific kind of end or goal, and not the having of an end or goal as such, that makes it a living thing. For as we saw in earlier chapters, even non-biological phenomena can be teleological or governed by the principle of finality. It is *immanent* teleology or finality that is definitive of life.

From the Aristotelian point of view, there are certain features of life which we simply cannot adequately describe or understand unless we think in terms of immanent causality. To borrow an example from Pasnau and Shields, when a snake eats and digests a gerbil, we naturally say that part of the gerbil has now become part of the snake (with the rest defecated away) and not that the snake has become part of the gerbil or that snake and gerbil have become a hybrid. The reason is that it is obvious that the process in question involves the nourishing and benefiting *of the snake* specifically, not of the gerbil and not of some new snake–gerbil hybrid. After all, the snake still exists while the gerbil is gone, and this is true even if before it digests the gerbil the snake vomits it up and never incorporates it into itself at all (lest someone seriously wants to entertain the "hybrid" idea). It will not do to try to describe the situation entirely in terms of bits of matter pushing or pulling one another in more or less complex patterns, after the fashion of transeunt causation. The digestive causal processes taking place within the snake are *immanent* and simply not reducible to the sort of causal relationship holding between the snake and the soil it displaces as it slithers along the ground, say, or even between raindrops, grains of sand, or crystals as they form hurricanes, sandstorms, and lattices respectively. Hence from the Aristotelian point of view they are not susceptible of purely mechanistic explanation – a conclusion reinforced by the various considerations considered in the previous two chapters in favor of the continuing relevance to biology of the notion of final causality.

Now machines, or at least complex machines, might seem to exhibit immanent causation of the sort definitive of life. We say, for example, that a coffee machine can turn itself on in the morning, that computers can run self-diagnostic routines, and so forth. So, could machines count as living things on Aquinas's view, and thus as having souls? They could not. For a living thing is a kind of substance, but machines are artifacts. And though an artifact can be described in a loose sense as if it were a kind of substance (as we did in chapter 2 when using examples like the rubber ball), in the *strict* sense an artifact is not a genuine substance at all, in Aquinas's view, but rather a composite of substances, or of parts of substances (*In DA* II.1.218; *SCG*

IV.35.7). This is evident from the fact that the parts of an artifact have no inherent tendency to come together and function as a coffee machine, or computer, or whatever, but have to be arranged *by us* to do so. Their inherent tendencies are rather to behave as the kinds of things they naturally are, or as the parts of the natural things they were once parts of. To take an example from Aristotle, if a wooden bed could be planted (while the wood was still fresh from the original tree, say) what would grow from it, if anything, would be a tree and not a bed (Aristotle, *Physics* Book II, Chapter 1; cf. *In Phys* II.2.149). The wood's arrangement as a bed is accidental, not essential or substantial. But the same is true of the parts of a machine, in which case no machine, or any human artifact generally, could possibly have the immanent causal processes definitive of life, but at most only a man-made simulacrum of such processes.

If machines cannot have souls, it should be obvious from what has been said already that plants and non-human animals can and do have them, for they are living things and a soul is just the form of a living thing. But that does not mean that when your favorite rose bush or cat dies its soul goes to heaven. Like the forms of rocks and water droplets, the souls of plants and animals are mere abstractions considered by themselves, apart from the matter they inform, so that when the plant or animal goes, its soul goes with it. (Things are different with the soul of a human being, as we will see later on.)

The soul of a plant is the kind Aristotelians traditionally call a *vegetative* or *nutritive* soul, which is just that kind of form which gives the thing that has it the powers of taking in nutrients, growing, and reproducing itself (*In DA* II.7–9). The soul of a non-human animal is called a *sensory* or *animal* soul, and it is that which gives the thing that has it not only the powers of the vegetative soul, but in addition to those the powers of sensation, of locomotion, and of having the sorts of appetites associated with sensation and locomotion (*In DA* II.10ff.). That is to say, an animal can sense the world around it (by seeing, hearing, etc.), can move itself about independently (by walking, flying, or swimming, say), and can desire or be repulsed by the things it senses so as to move towards or away from them. The soul of a human being is called the *intellective* or *rational* soul, and it includes the powers of the vegetative and sensory souls, and adds to them the distinctively human powers of intellect and will: that is to say, the power to grasp abstract concepts and to reason on the basis of them, and freely to choose between different possible courses of action on the basis of what the intellect knows (*In DA* III.7ff.). The relationship between these three kinds of soul illustrates Aquinas's hierarchical conception of the structure of reality, which we described in chapter 2. The sensory soul incorporates but adds to the powers of the vegetative soul, and the intellective soul incorporates and adds to the powers of both the vegetative and the sensory souls, so that there is a natural hierarchical relationship between them. Moreover, the powers of each kind of soul higher up in the hierarchy are irreducible to those of the lower kinds of soul. This is particularly evident in the case of the intellective soul, as we will see presently.

Before doing so, however, let us briefly consider the questions of when the soul is first conjoined with the body and when it leaves, focusing on the case of most interest to human beings, namely human beings themselves. These questions appear deeply problematic given a Cartesian understanding of the soul as a kind of immaterial substance. For since, on that understanding, the soul is not only distinct from but utterly independent of the body, there is no special reason for it to become conjoined with the body at any particular moment. Hence it seems entirely possible for it to be absent during much or even all of the time of the body's gestation within the womb. Indeed, given Descartes' emphasis on *thinking* as of the essence of the soul, the earliest time it would seem to be *necessary* for the soul to be present would be whenever a human being can be judged to have actual thoughts with conceptual content, or at least to be capable of them – something that doesn't occur until well after birth. Even then, the question of *why* the soul gets conjoined to the body at that point (or at some earlier point – and which exactly?) seems difficult to answer. Given the radical independence of soul and body, there is nothing about the state of the body at least at its earliest stages that demands the presence of the soul. Similarly, the latest the soul would seem to be necessarily conjoined with the body would be whatever the latest point is at which a human being can be said to be thinking, or at least to be capable of doing so. And that might in principle be well before biological death occurs, such as when a person lapses into what is sometimes called a "persistent vegetative state." Obviously, this would seem to open the way in principle to the moral legitimacy of euthanasia and abortion (even infanticide!) in at least certain cases (though Descartes himself, it should be noted, did not draw these conclusions).

On an Aristotelian view, however, on which the soul is the form of the body – that is to say, that which makes the matter composing the body into a living body in the first place – there appears to be no special difficulty in saying when the soul is present in the body. It is present, and necessarily so, whenever the body itself is present. Hence, if (as current biological knowledge indicates) the human organism comes into being at conception, then from an Aristotelian point of view it would seem to follow that that is necessarily when the soul is first present, otherwise it just wouldn't *be* a human organism, for the matter that makes it up wouldn't have the requisite form. Similarly, as long as the human body is alive, the soul must continue to be present, otherwise it just wouldn't be a living human body in the first place. (It would not be present after death, for even though the "body" is still present, it is not a *living* body, and the soul is the principle of life. Indeed, for

Aristotelians what exists after death is, *strictly* speaking, not someone's body, but only the remains of what used to be a body.) But if the soul, and thus the human being, is present from conception until death, then given that at least innocent human beings cannot justly be killed (an assumption Aquinas would certainly endorse), euthanasia, and abortion at any stage of pregnancy, would be ruled out as immoral.

It is true, of course, that fetuses and persons with severe brain damage do not exercise the powers distinctive of the rational soul, namely intellect and will. But for Aquinas, that would not suffice to show that they do not have those powers, or in general that they do not have rational souls. Recall from chapter 2 that from an Aristotelian point of view, what is essential to a thing remains essential to it even if it is somehow prevented from manifesting itself. Triangles essentially have three straight sides and angles adding up to 180 degrees even though some poorly drawn triangles do not perfectly instantiate these features. Dogs are essentially four-legged even though injury or genetic defect might leave some particular dog with only three. And human beings are essentially rational animals even though human beings who are not yet fully formed and those who have been damaged might be prevented from manifesting their rationality. But a badly drawn triangle still has the form of a triangle, however imperfectly, and a defective dog still has the form of a dog; otherwise they would not be triangles or dogs in the first place. Similarly, an immature or damaged human being still has the form of a human being, and thus a soul, otherwise he or she wouldn't be human in the first place.

Now while Aquinas himself did regard the killing of an "animated foetus" as homicide (*ST* II-II.64.8), he did not in fact hold that the soul is present from the moment of conception (which is why he refers to an "*animated* foetus," i.e. one in which the soul *is* present). Rather, he held that the composite of semen and menstrual blood which (as he saw it, given the biological knowledge then available) is the immediate product of conception had to pass through several stages before a body could be formed capable of being informed by an intellective soul (*SCG* II.89). Though he nevertheless regarded abortion as immoral at any stage from conception onward, he would have allowed that at the earliest stage it would not amount to homicide, but only to the lesser sin of contraception. (We will see why Aquinas regarded contraception as immoral in the next chapter.)

Robert Pasnau has suggested that this shows that Aquinas's understanding of the soul tends to imply, all by itself, that ensoulment can occur only much later than conception. But as John Haldane and Patrick Lee have argued in response (and in line with what I suggested above), when combined with what we know from modern biology, Aquinas's view of the soul actually seems to entail that the soul is present from conception onward, and that it is only Aquinas's ignorance of the relevant biological facts that led him to a different conclusion. Pasnau's position assumes that on a Thomistic view, the intellective soul could be present only once bodily organs have developed to a point sufficient to allow for the immediate possibility of conceptual thought, and that to suggest otherwise implies the implausible and certainly un-Thomistic view that the intellective soul could in principle be present in any material body whatever. But as Haldane and Lee point out, a third alternative is that the intellective soul is present once what they call the "epigenetic primordia" of the organs in question are present, which they are from the beginning insofar as within the first two days after conception cells begin to differentiate in the direction of the development of the nervous system, eyes, and so on. Moreover, since what is present from conception (and certainly long before the brain and other organs are well developed) is the beginnings of a specifically human body, and since development from conception onward is governed by genetic factors internal to the organism itself, it is not only possible but *necessary* on a Thomistic analysis that a human (and thus intellective) soul is present. Finally, Pasnau's view would also have the bizarre (and definitely un-Thomistic) consequence that a six-week-old infant cannot count as a human organism, since it is not yet capable of conceptual thought.

Intellect and will

We noted that Aquinas regards the human soul as sitting atop a hierarchy of kinds of soul. Part of its superiority lies in the fact that each higher kind of soul incorporates and adds to the powers of the lower ones; a higher soul can do everything a lower one can, and more. But there is more to its superiority than the quantity of its functions. Like other natural objects and processes, organisms and their activities are ordered to certain ends as their final causes, and these ends too have a hierarchical structure. A plant is ordered by nature towards the taking in of nutrients, growth, and reproduction. An animal has these natural ends too, along with the ends entailed by its distinctive powers of sensation, locomotion, and appetite. But notice that some of these ends are subordinated to the others. The point of taking in nutrients, for example, is to enable a plant or animal to carry out its other functions, such as growing and reproducing (*In DA* II.9.347).

Now a human being has all these ends too, but in addition has intellect and will, each with their own distinctive natural ends. The natural end or final cause of the intellect, with its capacity to grasp abstract concepts and to reason on the basis of them, is to attain truth (*In Meta* I.1.2–3). The natural end of the will is to choose those courses of action which best accord with the truth as it is discovered by the intellect, and in particular in accordance with the truth about human nature. (This, as we will see in the next chapter, is precisely what morality is in Aquinas's view: the habitual choice of actions which further the hierarchically ordered natural ends inherent in human nature.) But the intellect's capacity to know the truth is more fully realized the deeper is its understanding of the nature of the world and the causes underlying it; and in Aquinas's view the deepest truth about the world is, as we saw in chapter 3, that it is caused and sustained in being by God. Hence the highest fulfillment of the human intellect is to know God (*ST* I-II.1.8); and since the will's natural end is to choose in a way that facilitates the realization of our natural ends as human beings, the highest fulfillment of free choice is to live in a way that facilitates the knowing of God. All the vegetative and sensory powers of the soul are subordinated to these distinctive and overarching ends of the intellect and will (*ST* I.91.3). Though on the first level of analysis the human soul is just the form of the human body, it thus turns out on deeper analysis to have a divine purpose which raises it far above plant and animal souls in dignity.

Intellect and will are, then, the keys to the human soul's superiority; it is by virtue of these distinctive powers that human beings are, unlike other animals, made in the image of God (*ST* I.3.1; *ST* I.93.6). Their natural ends or final causes are, as I have just indicated, part of the reason, and we will return to that subject in the next chapter. But another reason has to do with their irreducibility to the lower functions of the soul. For Aquinas, intellect differs from sensation not just in degree, but in kind; and the difference between the will and merely animal appetite is similarly absolute.

Let us begin with the nature of the intellect. That it is irreducible to sensation is evident from the fact that "sense is cognizant only of singulars" while "the intellect is cognizant of universals, as experience proves" (*SCG* II.66.3; cf. *ST* I.12.4). Through seeing, hearing, tasting, touching, and smelling, we can only perceive *individual, particular* things: this triangle, that cat, and so forth. But the intellect can grasp triangularity in general, "catness" in general, and other universals, as essences which apply to indefinitely many individuals. Moreover, "sense-cognition is limited to corporeal things," while "the intellect knows incorporeal things, such as wisdom, truth, and the relations of things" (*SCG* II.66.4). That is to say, abstractions like the ones Aquinas mentions are not physical objects, but the intellect is nevertheless capable of entertaining them, while the senses can only ever perceive physical things.

Now sensation gives rise to imagination: the visual, auditory, gustatory, tactile, and olfactory perceptions we have are recalled in mental images or "phantasms" (as Aquinas calls them). Early modern empiricist philosophers like Berkeley and Hume held that intellect could be reduced to imagination. But for Aquinas, this is as impossible as reducing intellect to sensation, for like the senses, "imagination has to do with bodily and singular things only," while "the intellect … grasps objects universal and incorporeal" (*SCG* II.67.3). And it is notoriously difficult to defend the empiricists against this objection. Any mental image is always going to be particular and individual in some respect, in a way that the concepts grasped by the intellect are not. For example, the mental image you form of a triangle is necessarily going to be of an equilateral, isosceles, or scalene triangle specifically; but the concept of a triangle that your intellect grasps is one that applies to all of these, precisely because it abstracts away from these properties. Hence your concept of a triangle cannot be identified with a mental image. Mental images are also often vague and indistinct in a way that concepts are not. To repeat an earlier example, you can form no clear mental image of a chiliagon – a 1,000-sided figure – certainly not one that is distinct from your mental image of a 997-sided figure, or for that matter from your mental image of a circle. Still, the intellect can easily distinguish the concept of a chiliagon from the concept of a 997-sided figure and the concept of a circle. There are certain things we can form no mental images of – abstractions like law, love, and economics, the absence of a thing, and so forth – but the intellect can easily form concepts of them. And so on. Thus, as Aquinas argues, the intellect is as irreducible to the imagination as it is to sensation.

At the same time, "the operation of the intellect has its origin in the senses" (*ST* I.78.4), and "in the present state of life in which the soul is united to a passible body, it is impossible for our intellect to understand anything actually, except by turning to the phantasms" (*ST* I.84.7). That is to say, though the intellect is distinct from sensation and imagination, it depends upon them for its raw materials. In explaining what this involves, Aquinas, following Aristotle, draws a distinction between *agent intellect* (or "active intellect") and *possible intellect* (or "passive intellect"). Sensation involves perceptions of individual things, which give rise to the images or phantasms of the imagination and memory. The visual perception you have of a cat, for example, is later recalled in the mental image you have of what the cat looked like, and your imagination is also able to produce images of cats you have never seen by rearranging the elements of your mental images of things you have seen. But all such images or phantasms are, as we have said, particular or individual, just as the original perceptions and the things perceived were; and as such they are not "intelligible," that is to say, they are not the sort of thing the intellect can grasp. But "the active intellect ... causes the phantasms received from the senses to be actually intelligible, by a process of abstraction" (*ST* I.84.6). In other words, it strips away all particularizing or individualizing features of a phantasm so as to produce a truly universal concept or "intelligible species," leaving you (for instance) with the idea not just of this or that particular cat, but of "catness" in general, of that which is common to all cats. The abstract concept is then stored in the possible intellect (*ST* I.85.1). This account of the origin of our concepts is intended by Aristotle and Aquinas to serve as a middle position between two erroneous extremes: the materialism of ancient thinkers like Democritus, which in its overemphasis on the sensory origin of our concepts tended to identify intellect with sensation; and the hyper-intellectualism of Plato, who, though he correctly distinguished the intellect from the senses, tended too radically to divorce the former from the latter, and to cut off the intellect from the material world altogether (*ST* I.84.6).

Aquinas's talk of "phantasms," "intelligible species," and the like may give the impression that he is committed to some form of indirect realism, the view that all we ever directly perceive are subjective mental representations, and know of external material objects only by inference from these representations. But nothing could be further from the truth, and Aquinas is very much a direct realist, holding that in perception it is the objects themselves that the mind grasps and not merely representations of them. The role the mental items in question do play is summarized by Aquinas as follows:

> The intelligible species is to the intellect what the sensible image is to the sense. But the sensible image is not what is perceived, but rather that *by which* sense perceives. Therefore the intelligible species is not what is actually understood, but that *by which* the intellect understands. (*ST* I.85.2, emphasis added)

When you see a cat, it is true that you have a perceptual representation or "sensible image" of the cat in your mind. But what you perceive really is the cat itself, and not the representation, which is merely that "by which" you perceive the cat in the sense of being the medium through which perception takes place. To use an imperfect analogy, if you need glasses in order to see the cat, you might say that the glasses are also something "by which" you see it; but it is still the cat you see, and not the glasses, which are only a means of helping you to see it. Similarly, when you think about cats in general, you do so by having the concept *cat* in your intellect. But what you are thinking *about* are cats themselves, not your concept of them.

Especially in the case of concepts, it would from the Aristotelian–Thomistic point of view be very misleading to think of them as "representations" in the first place, as contemporary philosophers of mind tend to do. The conception of the mind modern philosophy inherited from Descartes and Locke portrays thoughts, sensations, and other mental items as objects analogous to the words, pictures, and other representations familiar from everyday experience, but having a subjective rather than objective mode of existence. That is to say, unlike literal, physical words and pictures, which can be known through the five senses by any observer, these mental objects are taken to be directly knowable only by the thinkers in whose minds they exist. This gives rise to the idea that what we are directly aware of are just the subjective mental representations themselves, which notoriously opens the door to the problem of explaining how, if this is so, we can ever have knowledge of a real physical world beyond our representations. It also generates the problem of "intentionality." This is the feature of our mental states by virtue of which they represent or "point to" something beyond themselves (as your thought about cats represents or "points beyond itself" to cats). We know that literal, physical words and pictures can represent things (and thus have a kind of intentionality) despite being in themselves otherwise meaningless squiggles of ink or patterns of color, because *we* impart meaning to them by using them to convey our thoughts and ideas. But where does the intentionality that characterizes our own minds come from? If the representations outside the mind get their meanings from the representations inside the mind, where do the latter get *their* meaning?

From an Aristotelian–Thomistic point of view, this whole way of characterizing the mind's relationship to the external world is wrongheaded from the start. For the intellect to have a concept is not for it to have something analogous to a little picture or word in the mind, a kind of internal subjective entity which "represents" another, external, objective entity. Rather, when the intellect understands something, it grasps its form. And that means that *one and the same thing*, namely the form of the thing understood, exists both in the intellect and in the thing itself. For example, when you understand what a triangle is, the form of triangularity which exists in actual triangles now exists also in your intellect; when you understand what cats are, the form of "catness" which exists in actual cats now exists also in your intellect; and so forth. There are not two things, a subjective representation (of a triangle, cat, or whatever) and an external object (the actual cat or triangle), which would raise the question of how the one gets in contact with or represents the other. There is just *one* thing, a form, which (again to make use of Scholastic terminology) exists in two ways, an "entitative" way (in this case, as instantiated in matter so as to comprise with it a material object) and an "intentional" way (that is, in the intellect).

For this reason, Aquinas, following Aristotle, holds that "the soul is in a way all things" (*In DA* III.13.787), a startling claim that John Haldane has labeled the "mind-world identity theory." But the qualifier "in a way" is obviously important. Aquinas is not claiming that the intellect *is* or *is identical with* the things it thinks about, without qualification; obviously your mind is not the same thing as a triangle or a cat, for example. His point is rather that it is of the essence of the intellect that one and the very same thing, a form, exists both in it and in the real world when the former knows the latter:

> Intelligent beings are distinguished from non-intelligent beings in that the latter possess only their own form; whereas the intelligent being is naturally adapted to have also the form of some other thing; for the idea of the thing known is in the knower. (*ST* I.14.1)

Had he been familiar with the modern philosophical problem of bridging the (epistemological and representational) gap between mind and reality, Aquinas would no doubt have said that no such gap can arise when the nature of the intellect is rightly understood.

Let us turn now to the will. The first thing to note about it is that "in every intellectual being there is will, just as in every sensible being there is animal appetite," for "will follows upon intellect" (*ST* I.19.1). On the Aristotelian doctrine of final causes, the inclination or tendency towards an end pervades the natural order. In animals this inclination or tendency can take the form of sensory appetites, insofar as animals can be moved towards that which they apprehend through the senses (*ST* I.81.1). And it can take the form of what we call will in the case of beings with intellects, in that they can be moved towards that which they *rationally* apprehend. That is just what will is on Aquinas's account: a power to be drawn towards (or away from) that which is apprehended by the intellect (*SCG* IV.19). (More precisely, it is the power to be drawn towards or away from that which is apprehended to be good or bad, respectively, but we will wait until chapter 5 to explain this qualification.) It follows automatically that that which lacks intellect (as lower animals do) cannot have will, free or otherwise.

Now a question suggested by our discussion of the argument from motion in chapter 3 is whether *our* wills can in fact be free. For if God is the first mover underlying all the motion or change that takes place in the world, that would have to include the motion or change that results from our voluntary actions, in which case God must be the ultimate cause of those actions. But in that case, how can they be free actions? Aquinas considers this question himself (*QDM* 6; cf. *ST* I.83.1). His answer is that though God does move the will, "since he moves every kind of thing according to the nature of the moveable thing ... he also moves the will according to its condition, as indeterminately disposed to many things, not in a necessary way" (*QDM* 6). That is to say, the nature of the will is to be open to various possible intellectually apprehended ends, while something unfree, like an impersonal physical object or process, is naturally determined to its ends in an unthinking, necessary way. When you choose to have coffee rather than tea, you could have done otherwise, whereas when the coffee maker heated your coffee, it could not have done otherwise. This is so because your will was the cause of your having coffee, while something outside the coffee machine – your having keyed certain instructions into it the night before, say, together with the electrical current passing into it from the wall socket, the laws of physics, and so forth – was the cause of its behavior. But God causes both events in a manner consistent with all of this, insofar as in causing your free choice he causes something that operates independently of what happens in the world around you, while in causing the coffee machine to heat the coffee he causes something that operates only in virtue of what is happening in the world around it (the electricity, laws of physics, etc.). In this way God causes each thing to act in accordance with its nature. Aquinas summarizes his position as follows:

> Free-will is the cause of its own movement, because by his free-will man moves himself to act. But it does not of necessity belong to liberty that what is free should be the first cause of itself, as neither for one thing to be cause of another need it be the first cause. God, therefore, is the first cause, Who moves causes both natural and voluntary. And just as by moving natural causes He does not prevent their acts being natural, so by moving voluntary causes he does not deprive their actions of being voluntary: but rather is He the cause of this very thing in them; for He operates in each thing according to its own nature. (*ST* I.83.1)

As this passage indicates, for Aquinas what matters to freedom is whether the cause of one's behavior is something in the external natural world (as it is for natural objects themselves) or rather one's own will. That God is the ultimate cause of both the will and the natural causal order does not undermine freedom; indeed, it makes it possible in the sense that just as with natural causes, if free choices were not caused by God, they couldn't exist at all.

Immateriality and immortality

The operations of the vegetative and sensory souls depend entirely on matter for their operation. For example, a plant cannot carry out photosynthesis without leaves, and an animal cannot digest its meal without a stomach. This is why the souls of plants and animals cannot survive the destruction of their bodies (*ST* I.75.3). Naturally, the vegetative and sensory functions of the human soul also depend on matter. Even phantasms or mental images, which might seem to post-Cartesian philosophers of mind to be paradigmatically ghostly and immaterial, are in Aquinas's view dependent on the existence of bodily organs (*ST* I.85.1). However, the intellect, and the will insofar as it follows on the intellect, are different. These are in Aquinas's view essentially *immaterial*, not requiring any bodily organ for their operation. This not only adds to the dignity of the human soul of which they are the distinctive powers, but entails that that soul alone has a kind of natural immortality.

Aquinas gives a number of arguments for the intellect's independence from matter. (*SCG* II.49–51 summarizes quite a few of them.) But two arguments in particular seem to have gotten the most attention from commentators, and they do appear to have been regarded as especially important by Aquinas himself. Both arguments suggest that it is the nature of the intellect's distinctive objects – the forms of things, understood as abstracted universals or "intelligible species" – that most clearly reveals its immateriality. The first is as follows:

> By means of the intellect man can have knowledge of all corporeal things. Now whatever knows certain things cannot have any of them in its own nature; because that which is in it naturally would impede the knowledge of anything else. Thus we observe that a sick man's tongue being vitiated by a fever-ish and bitter humor, is insensible to anything sweet, and every-thing seems bitter to it. Therefore, if the intellectual principle contained the nature of a body it would be unable to know all bodies. (*ST* I.75.2; cf. *In DA* III.7.680 and *QDA* 14)

Aquinas describes this as the "main reason" why the intellect is immaterial (*QDA* 14). But especially for modern readers, it may not be obvious at first glance what the argument is.

One possible reading would focus on the claim that the intel-lect can know "*all* corporeal things." The example of the "sick man's tongue," as well as another illustration Aquinas gives later in the same passage to the effect that the presence of a certain color in the eye might make a liquid one is looking at seem to be of that color, would then seem to indicate that what Aquinas is getting at is this: when a sensory organ is "biased" in its perceptions in a certain direction, there are certain things it is incapable of perceiving. To a tongue coated with a bitter substance everything will taste somewhat bitter, so that at least some sweet substances will be undetectable to it. To eyes wearing green contact lenses, everything will seem to take on at least a faint green hue, so that certain shades of color will be invisible to them. But if the intellect depended on some mater-ial organ for its operation, then it would be "biased" in the direction of that kind of matter in just the way the tongue and eyes in question are biased in the direction of bitterness and greenness. And in that case there would be certain material things whose natures it could not grasp, just as there are certain tastes and colors that the tongue and eyes of our examples cannot perceive. But the intellect is not limited in the sorts of material natures it can grasp. Therefore it must not depend on the operation of any material organ.

Certainly this argument is clear. But it is also obvious that it might be challenged on several fronts. How do we know, for example, that the intellect can grasp the natures of *all* material things? Maybe there are some that it cannot grasp, and if so, this might be precisely because it depends on a certain kind of material organ itself. And is the analogy between the intellect and the senses close enough in the first place to justify the inference that a material intellect would be biased in a way that prevented the grasp of certain material natures?

It seems to me, however, that this interpretation of Aquinas's argument doesn't get to the heart of it. In particular, and as parallel texts seem to imply, the argument does not in fact crucially depend on the claim that the intellect can understand *every* kind of material thing, and the "bias" that matter would impose on the intellect does not crucially depend on the analogy with sense organs. The force of the argument depends instead on the way in which, as we have seen, the intellect takes on the form of the thing it understands in the very act of understanding it. This capacity shows that the intellect has "potencies" which material things do not have (*In DA* III.7.680), and in particular that the intellect can, unlike material things, take on the form of other things (whether all of them or only some is irrelevant) without losing its own form (*SCG* II.49.3).

When understood in light of his general account of what intellectual activity involves, what Aquinas is saying in the specific argument in question seems, then, to be something like this: when the intellect grasps the form of a thing, it is necessarily *one and the same* form that exists both in the thing itself and in the intellect. The form of triangularity that exists in our intellects when we think about triangles is *one and the same* form that exists in actual triangles themselves; the form of "catness" that exists in our intellects when we think about cats is *one and the same* form that exists in actual cats; and so forth. If this weren't the case, then we wouldn't really be thinking of triangles, cats, and so on in the first place, since to think about these things requires grasping what they are, and what they are is determined by their forms. Now suppose that the intellect were a material thing (some kind of brain activity, say). Then for the forms of our example to exist in the intellect would be for them to exist in a certain material thing. But for a form to exist in a material thing is just for that material thing to be the kind of thing the form is a form of. For example, for the form of triangularity to exist in a certain parcel of matter is just for that parcel of matter to be a triangle; for the form of "catness" to exist in a certain parcel of matter is just for that parcel of matter to be a cat; and so on. Thus, if your intellect were really a material thing, it would follow that that material thing – that part of your brain, say – would become a triangle whenever you thought about triangles, or a cat whenever you thought about cats. But of course, that's absurd. Hence, since the assumption that the intellect is material leads to such absurdity, we must conclude that the intellect is not material.

Indeed, if the intellect were material and thus became a cat when thinking about cats, it could never think about anything else ever again (whether triangles or whatever) since it would in that case not exist anymore – the parcel of matter composing it, having now become a cat, would no longer be an intellect at all (which seems to be Aquinas's point in the passage cited from *SCG* II.49.3). Similarly, if the intellect were material it could never think about cats and triangles *at the same time*, for in taking on their forms (as it does in grasping them) it would then *become* both a cat and a triangle at the same time, which of course nothing can be. This, I would suggest, is what Aquinas means by saying that if the intellect were material, its knowing one thing "would impede the knowledge of anything else." The point is not so much that the intellect can know *all* material things, but rather that it can know enough of them to justify us in inferring that it cannot be material. Indeed, just knowing that it can grasp both triangles and cats suffices to justify this inference. Insofar as it can take on the forms of multiple things, both over time and at a particular moment, the intellect has a potency that nothing material has or can have.

The second of Aquinas's main arguments for the immateriality of the intellect is as follows:

> from the fact that the human soul knows the universal natures of things, [philosophers] have perceived that the species by which we understand is immaterial. Otherwise, it would be individuated and so would not lead to knowledge of the universal. From the immateriality of the species by which we understand, philosophers have understood that the intellect is a thing independent of matter. (*QDV* X.8; cf. *ST* I.75.5 and *DEE* 4)

Precisely by virtue of being universal, the objects of the intellect are not material, for all material things are particular rather than universal. This or that individual triangle is a material thing, but the universal *triangularity* is not; this or that individual cat is a material thing, but the universal *catness* is not; and so on. If *triangularity*, say, were a material thing, then our knowledge of it would be knowledge of just one particular material thing among others and thus not knowledge of a universal at all. That much is relatively uncontroversial. But how does it follow that the intellect which grasps these immaterial universal natures is *itself* immaterial?

One basis for this inference that we might suggest on Aquinas's behalf would be that if the intellect were material, then its operation would presumably involve some purely material process, such as the manipulation of formal symbols a la modern "computational" accounts of the mind. In that case a thought about *triangularity*, for example, would consist of some physical representation of *triangularity* in the brain somewhere (in the form of a neuronal firing pattern or whatever). But no such physical representation could possibly count as the universal *triangularity*, because like any other physical representation of a triangle, this one too would be just one particular material thing among others, and not universal at all. Thus the operations of the intellect cannot consist of purely material processes.

Another basis for the inference from the immateriality of the objects of the intellect to the immateriality of the intellect itself is one suggested by James Ross. When you think about *triangularity*, as you might when proving a geometrical theorem, it is necessarily *perfect* triangularity that you are contemplating, not some approximation of it. *Triangularity* as your intellect grasps it is entirely determinate or exact. (Of course, your mental image of a triangle might not be exact, but rather indeterminate and fuzzy; but as we've seen, to grasp something with the intellect is not the same as to form a mental image of it.) Now the thought you are having must be as determinate or exact as *triangularity* itself, otherwise it just wouldn't *be* a thought about *triangularity* in the first place, but only a thought about some approximation of triangularity. Yet material things are never determinate or exact in this way. Any material triangle, for example, is always only ever an approximation of perfect triangularity (since it is bound to have sides that are less than perfectly straight, etc., even if this is undetectable to the naked eye). And in general, material symbols and representations are inherently always to some extent vague, ambiguous, or otherwise inexact, susceptible of various alternative interpretations. It follows, then, that any thought you might have about *triangularity* is not something material; in particular, it is not some process occurring in the brain. And what goes for *triangularity* goes for any thought that involves the grasp of a universal, since universals in general (or at least very many of them, in case someone should wish to dispute this) are determinate and exact in a way material objects and processes cannot be.

Whatever one thinks of arguments like this, it is important to understand that they are not the sort that might be undermined by the findings of neuroscience, or any other empirical science for that matter. They are not "soul of the gaps" arguments any more than Aquinas's arguments for God's existence are "God of the gaps" arguments. That is to say, Aquinas is not presenting a quasi-scientific explanation of some psychological phenomenon that we simply haven't got enough empirical data to explain in a materialistic way. As with the Five Ways, he is attempting to provide a metaphysical demonstration. He is claiming that it is *in principle* impossible, *conceptually* impossible for the intellect to be accounted for in a materialistic way. If his arguments work at all, they establish conclusively that the intellect could no more be identified with processes in the brain than two and two could make five. If they are mistaken, they would be mistaken in the way one might make a mistake in attempting to carry out a geometrical proof, and not by virtue of having failed to take account of this or that finding of brain research.

The immateriality of the intellect has several consequences for Aquinas's overall system of thought. For the reasons just stated, material things cannot possess more than one form precisely because they are material, and intellects can do so precisely because they are not. But that is what the intellect's having knowledge of things amounts to: its possession of a thing's form without itself being that thing. Aquinas infers from this that the farther a thing is from materiality – the further it is up the hierarchy of reality that extends from prime matter at the bottom to pure act at the top – the more it is capable of having knowledge. And that is ultimately why God, as pure act, must be all knowing (*ST* I.14.1).

In showing that the human intellect is immaterial, Aquinas

takes himself to have shown also that the human soul is, unlike the souls of plants and animals, a "subsistent" form (*ST* I.75.2). That is to say, it has its being, and (in part) its operation, in itself, independent of anything else, including the body. For even when it is conjoined to the body, its intellectual and volitional acts, being independent of any material organ, are undertaken independently of the body. And what can operate independently must exist independently, since "a thing operates according as it is; for which reason we do not say that heat imparts heat, but that what is hot gives heat" (*ST* I.75.2). In other words, heat all by itself cannot heat anything because it is a mere accident rather than a substance, and therefore cannot even exist on its own; but a coal that is hot, since it is a substance, can heat something else. Similarly, intellectual activity cannot exist all by itself but requires a subject, and since that subject operates apart from matter it must be an immaterial subject. Of course, given Aquinas's account of the origin of our concepts, the intellect requires sensation and the phantasms it gives rise to in order to abstract from them the "intelligible species" or abstract universals that it grasps; and these in turn require bodily organs (eyes, ears, the brain, etc.). But once this abstraction has occurred, the soul's intellectual operations can carry on independently of matter.

Because it is subsistent, the human soul is capable, unlike plant and animal souls and indeed unlike the forms of all other material things, of existing apart from the matter it informs. In particular, it is capable of surviving the death of the body. Here Aquinas goes beyond Aristotle, who, though he was clear that the intellect is at least partially immaterial, was not clear about whether the individual intellect persisted beyond death. Still, Aquinas's arguments are Aristotelian in spirit. Material things perish precisely because they lose their forms; for example, a tree tossed into the wood chipper goes out of existence precisely because the matter that once comprised it has lost the form of a tree and taken on the form of wood chips. But a form itself is obviously not capable of losing its form, since it is a form. It is not the sort of thing it makes sense to speak of going out of existence; as we saw in chapter 2, for Aquinas it is composites of form and matter, rather than form and matter themselves, that are generated and corrupted. Of course, this does not entail that the forms of things which depend entirely on matter for their operation somehow carry on as individual substances beyond the deaths of the things they are the forms of, because apart from those things the forms are mere abstractions. But a *subsistent* form, one which already operates as a particular, concrete thing apart from matter even when it is conjoined with the thing it is the form of, is a different story. In its case, the fact that "it is impossible for a form to be separated from itself" (which it would have to do in order to perish) entails that "it is impossible for a subsistent form to cease to exist," so that it must carry on as a particular thing even beyond the death of the body it informs (*ST* I.75.6).

This is not meant by Aquinas to imply that it is impossible in an *absolute* sense for the human soul to go out of existence. For like everything else that exists other than God, even an immaterial substance is a composite of essence and existence, and thus can only continue to exist so long as God keeps it in being. At the same time, *only* God could cause the soul to perish. Given its nature, there is nothing *in the natural order* that could do so, and in that sense it has a kind of natural immortality, which material things, capable as they are of being destroyed by other material things, do not have.

Now it is sometimes suggested that Aquinas's position conflicts with his rejection of Platonic realism. Plato's view was that forms exist in a realm of their own, independently of the material world. Aristotle's moderate version of realism denies this, holding that forms exist only in the things they are the forms of. Aquinas is supposed to be an Aristotelian. So how can he consistently hold that the human soul, which is a kind of form, can subsist apart from the matter it informs? As we saw in chapter 2, Anthony Kenny raises precisely this objection to Aquinas's account of angels as pure forms. But as we also saw there, the objection fails insofar as it falsely assumes that Aquinas is affirming that forms can exist apart from matter *in the same sense* in which Plato thought they did. A Platonic Form is supposed to be abstract and universal on the one hand, and at the same time a kind of individual substance alongside other individual substances on the other. This is what makes the notion objectionable. But for Aquinas a human soul, like an angel, is a concrete (though immaterial) particular with its own individual act of existing, not a universal. Furthermore, there is for Aristotle an asymmetry between act and potency insofar as act can exist without potency even though potency cannot exist without act. It should hardly be surprising, then, that form (which is a kind of act) might exist without matter even though matter (a kind of potency) cannot exist without form. (This is not the normal case, of course, but then act usually doesn't exist without potency either.) Indeed, Aristotle himself allowed at least the *possibility* of the rational soul continuing to exist beyond the death of the body; he did not dismiss the idea as inherently absurd (*Metaphysics* Book XII, Chapter 3; cf. *In Meta* XII.3.2451). At the end of the day, then, the charge that Aquinas is a kind of Platonizing backslider, less than consistent in his Aristotelianism, seems not to hold up.

Moreover, though Aquinas regards the human soul as subsistent, he does not think of it as a substance in an unqualified way, but rather as a kind of incomplete substance (*ST* I.75.2; *QDA* 1). It is comparable in this respect to a hand or a foot, which, though they might subsist on their own for a time after being severed from the body (as is evident from the fact that they can sometimes be reattached), are nevertheless only parts of a substance (the human being as a whole) rather than complete substances in their own right. And like a hand or foot, the soul by itself is not a person; "soul is not the whole human being, only part of one: my soul is not me" (*In I Cor* 15). Aquinas's conception of the soul is thus very different from that of Plato or Descartes, for whom soul and body are each complete substances in their own right, with the soul being the true self, only contingently related to its body. For Aquinas, it is only the soul and body together which make up a complete substance, and a person. So close is their relationship that "there is no more reason to ask whether soul and body together make one thing than to ask the same about wax and the impression sealed on it, or about any other matter and its form" (*In DA* II.1.234).

Given that it is only soul and body together that constitute a person, the persistence of the soul after death does not amount to the survival of the person; when John dies, his *soul* carries on, but *he* does not, at least not strictly speaking. What the soul's survival does do, however, is make it *possible* for the person to live again. This would require the soul's being rejoined with the matter it once informed, and thus the resurrection of its body – something which cannot be accomplished naturally but only through divine intervention (*CT* I.154). But without the persistence of at least the soul after death, even divine intervention couldn't bring a person back. What makes a resurrection of a person's body a resurrection of that person, and not just the creation of a duplicate of the original person, is that there is continuity of the soul between death and resurrection.

Now since your soul is the form of your body specifically, it is precisely the same matter that made up your body to which it must be rejoined (*CT* I.153). It follows that on Aquinas's conception of the soul (unlike, presumably, Plato's or Descartes') neither the reincarnation of a human being's soul in a non-human animal's body, nor the entrance of one person's soul into the body of another (as in movies like *Freaky Friday*), would be possible even in principle. This also opens up Aquinas's position to the famous "cannibal problem": suppose a cannibal eats the body of another man and then, after his victim's flesh has been assimilated to his own body, the cannibal himself dies. Whose soul gets the matter in question at the resurrection? Aquinas's answer begins by noting that the matter comprising our bodies is always somewhat in flux in any case, as we take in new matter by eating and lose old matter through elimination and the like. Hence our resurrection does not require that every single bit of matter ever associated with our bodies be rejoined to our soul; indeed, if it did, then "the size of risen man would exceed all bounds" (*CT* I.159)! What is needed is "only so much as will be enough to constitute the species of the [body's] parts in integrity" (*CT* I.159); and even then, "the material elements existing in man's body are found to pertain to true human nature in various degrees" so that some bits of matter are bound to be more crucial to preserving identity than others (*CT* I.161). To take an obvious example (mine, not Aquinas's), not all of the body fat that exists in a certain person need be put back into his body in order to resurrect it. Hence in the case of the cannibal and his victim, the matter that is restored to the former need not be exactly that which he derived from the latter, but could instead be matter from things he ate previously; in a case where what he ate previously has primarily been other people, only such matter as goes into the more central elements of human nature need be restored to the cannibal and his victim in the first place; and where there is still a lack of matter despite the restoration of these bits, then just as in the normal course of things this is supplied from outside via eating and the like, so too can God supply it through his power (*CT* I.161; *SCG* IV.81.13).

Hylemorphic dualism

In their zeal to emphasize the differences between Aquinas's position and that of Plato and Descartes, some of his defenders have tended to insist that he was not only not a materialist, but not a dualist either. But this "pox on both houses" approach, motivated in part perhaps by a fear that contemporary philosophers might be too quick to dismiss Aquinas if he is labeled with the "D word," is not very plausible. As we have seen, Aquinas held both that the intellect is immaterial and that the soul survives the death of the body. Surely that counts as dualism by most people's reckoning, and certainly by the reckoning of most contemporary philosophers. To be sure, it is neither Cartesian dualism nor property dualism, the versions best known to contemporary philosophers. But it is dualism all the same: "Thomistic dualism," as some have called it, or "hylemorphic dualism," to borrow David Oderberg's apt coinage. Better, then, just frankly to acknowledge the fact, and to defend Aquinas's position on its merits rather than pretend it is something it is not.

Its merits, I would suggest, are in any event considerable. It is, after all, hardly as if dualism has no respectable defenders. The arguments that philosophers past and present have offered in its defense are many and powerful. (For those readers who are interested, I provide a detailed survey of them in my book *Philosophy of Mind: A Beginner's Guide*.) And while the particular versions of dualism mentioned above are open to several well-known objections, an advantage of Aquinas's hylemorphic dualism is that it is immune to them. Arguably, it affords us the benefits of dualism without the usual drawbacks.

Cartesian substance dualism holds, as has been said, that the mind or soul on the one hand and the body on the other constitute two complete substances rather than (as Aquinas's view does) two components of one complete substance. The body is defined in terms of the mechanistic conception of matter bequeathed to us by the early modern philosophers (and discussed in chapter 2), as inherently devoid of formal or final causes and operating entirely in terms of a stripped-down notion of efficient cause. The mind, apart from its being a thinking thing, is characterized in negative terms, by denying of it any of the properties typical of matter as mechanistically defined. In particular it has no length, width, depth, or position in space. Nevertheless, the mind is taken somehow to interact causally with the body. *How* a substance that has no length, width, depth, or position in space could get in any sort of cause and effect relationship with a material world defined in entirely quantificational terms is notoriously mysterious, however, and this "interaction problem" has always been the central objection to Cartesian dualism.

Property dualism denies that the mind is a non-physical substance of this sort. It accepts the materialist view that material substances (again, mechanistically defined) are the only substances there are. But it disagrees with materialism and agrees with Cartesian dualism in holding that mental *properties*, or at least some of them, are non-physical properties, and it takes these properties to inhere somehow in the physical substance of the brain. Some property dualists would include intentionality among these non-physical mental properties. The mental properties most property dualists focus on, however, are "qualia": those features of a conscious experience that are directly knowable only to the person having the experience and which are thus inherently subjective, such as the way colors look (which is different for someone with normal vision than it is for someone who is color blind), the way things taste (which is different for someone whose tongue is burnt than it is for someone whose tongue is in good working order), and so forth. The early modern philosophers and scientists who put forward a "mechanistic" conception of matter tended towards the view that colors, tastes, odors, sounds, and the like *as we subjectively experience them*, since they are qualitative rather than quantitative and vary from observer to observer, cannot be real features of material objects. For scientific purposes, then, color, and so on as *objective physical properties* were redefined in entirely quantifiable terms, and the residual elements of these properties that could not be captured in a quantifiable way were characterized as existing only in the mind, "sensory qualities" that we tend to project on to the physical world but which do not really exist there at all. The notion of "qualia" is the contemporary descendant of this early modern idea. Property dualism also faces a version of the interaction problem, insofar as the idea that non-physical properties could have any causal influence on the physical world is as mysterious as the idea that a non-physical substance could.

Now Aquinas would regard both these ways of looking at the relationship between mind and matter as deeply mistaken. The trouble, however, is not merely with their conception of the mind (as contemporary materialists assume it is) but also, and especially, with their conception of matter (a conception that materialists themselves are implicitly committed to). From an Aristotelian point of view, the mechanistic worldview is fundamentally wrongheaded, and its adoption is what created the so-called "mind–body problem" in the first place. For if matter is simply *defined* in such a way that formal and final causes are not allowed to count as physical, and only that which can be described in purely quantifiable terms *is* allowed to count as physical, then mental properties are *both* inevitably going to count as non-physical *and* seem impossible to relate causally to the physical world.

In particular, if it is held that material things are inherently devoid of anything like final causality or "directedness towards" an end, then *of course* intentionality (which involves the mind's being "directed towards" something beyond itself) is going to have to count as non-physical. And if that which cannot be captured entirely in mathematically quantifiable terms is not allowed to count as physical, then *of course* sensory qualities (and thus "qualia") must be regarded as non-physical. In the debate between contemporary materialists on the one hand and Cartesian and property dualists on the other, the Thomist is bound to regard the dualists as having the better of the argument. For contrary to what materialists tend complacently to suppose, dualism follows, not from ignorance of modern neuroscience or an unscientific attitude towards the world, but rather from *the very conception of matter they share in common with modern dualists*.

At the same time, this conception of matter also makes it difficult or even impossible for modern dualists to explain how the mental world can have any causal influence on the physical world. The main reason is not the dualist's conception of the mind as immaterial (again, contrary to what materialists suppose), but rather in the impoverished mechanistic understanding of the notions of substance and causation. In particular, it lies in the false assumption that the relationship between soul and body is to be conceived of as an instance of efficient causation between two complete substances. From the Thomistic point of view, the right way to think about this relationship is rather in hylemorphic terms, as an instance of *formal* causation relating two components of *one* complete substance. The body is not a complete substance, for matter can never exist all by itself. Matter only ever exists with some form or other, and the human body therefore exists only insofar as it has *its* form, that is to say, the rational soul. As the form of the body, the soul is not a complete substance either. It is only form and matter or soul and body together which constitute a complete substance, and they are related, not as one ghostly object somehow banging into another one, but rather in the way that the form of a table is related to the wood that makes it up, or the form of a dog is related to its flesh. Hence if those relationships are not particularly mysterious, neither is the relationship between soul and body.

One advantage of hylemorphic dualism, then, is that its notion of formal causation opens the way to acknowledging the immateriality of the soul while avoiding the interaction problem. A second, related advantage is that it arguably better accords with what we know from modern neuroscience about the close relationship between our mental lives and processes in the brain. To be sure, the Thomist would agree with the modern dualist that the case for the intellect's immateriality is not in the least affected by modern neuroscientific findings. We have already looked at the reasons for this. They have to do with the nature of intentionality, which is *in principle* impossible to account for in materialistic terms on either a hylemorphic conception of matter or a mechanistic one. In the former case, this is because nothing material can either possess the multiplicity of forms the intellect does or manifest the abstract universality and determinateness that at least many of our thoughts do. In the latter case, it is because nothing devoid of final causality can possess the directedness characteristic of intentionality.

Still, if intentionality exists in a realm totally divorced from matter (as Cartesian dualism claims), it is hard to see why there should be such a tight connection between specific mental processes and specific neurological ones. But this is not at all mysterious on a hylemorphic conception of the soul. For on such a conception, soul is related to body in a manner that is just as intimate as the relationship between the form of a table and the wood that makes it up. That is to say, just as there is no sense to be made of the wood of the table being just as it is (round, solid, etc.) without it having the form of a table, so too there is no sense to be made of the body, including its neurological states, being just as they are without their having a soul. The connection is a *necessary* one. Hence, to take a simple bodily action as an example, the intellect and will constitute the formal-cum-final cause of the action, of which the firing of the neurons, flexing of the muscles, and so on are the material-cum-efficient causes. That it is a *bodily* action is due to its matter and the way the bodily parts interact; that it is a bodily *action* with a certain specific end in view (rather than an involuntary reflex or an unconscious robotic movement) is due to its form and final cause. There are not (as there are for the Cartesian dualist) two substances with events going on in each that are somehow mysteriously correlated. There is *one* substance and *one* set of events having both formal and material, and final- and efficient-causal components.

This also gives the hylemorphic dualist an advantage over materialism, which has well-known problems of its own in explaining "mental causation." To avoid the interaction problem, the materialist identifies mental states with neurological ones. Hence your belief that it is raining can cause you to get your umbrella because the belief is just a certain neural process. So far so good. But the materialist also typically wants to say that it is only the physical properties of this process, and not the distinctively mental ones, that actually cause your body to move. That is to say, it is only the fact that the process has certain electrochemical properties, say, and not the fact that it represents rain or has any meaning at all, that is responsible for it causing your legs to move you over to the closet, and so forth. As with Cartesian dualism, it thus becomes mysterious even on a materialist view how the mind has any causal influence on the body. From the point of view of the Thomist, this is yet another bad consequence of the abandonment of the hylemorphic understanding of matter. But if we regard the neurological processes as the material- and efficient-causal side of a set of events of which the mental aspects are the formal- and final-causal side, the mystery disappears.

Then there is the issue of "qualia" or sensory qualities, which, I have suggested, inevitably count as non-material when the material world is defined in a mechanistic way, but which also seem in that case incapable of any causal interaction with the material world. On a hylemorphic understanding of matter, the mistake lies in the stipulation that only that which can be reduced to the mathematically quantifiable properties favored by modern physics can count as "material." For Aristotle and Aquinas, what modern philosophers call "sensory qualities" – whether that expression refers to qualities of external physical objects or to qualities of our experiences of them (there is a notorious ambiguity here) – are, though having a qualitative nature which cannot be cashed out in quantitative terms, just one set of material features of the world alongside others. It is no surprise at all, then, that there should be a close correlation between them and various physical properties. No doubt sensory qualities are unlike other features of the material world (size, shape, mass, electric charge, etc.), but from the Aristotelian–Thomistic point of view there is simply no good reason to think that all truly material attributes should be reducible to one, quantifiable, type in the first place. That assumption is (as Aristotelians and Thomists see it) just a bit of dogmatism on the part of modern philosophers who insist on making the world fit their method, rather than letting their method fit the world. The modern focus on sensory qualities (whether on the part of dualists or materialists) also radically distorts our understanding of the mind, falsely making it seem as if the sentience we share with non-human animals is the crucial and philosophically interesting phenomenon (as modern philosophers tend to assume), when in fact it is our intellects, which we do not share with them, that sets the mind (and thus us) apart from the rest of the material world (cf. *ST* I.75.3). From the Thomistic point of view, contemporary philosophers' obsession with the "qualia problem" is a red herring.

A third advantage of hylemorphic dualism is the light it arguably sheds on the philosophical problem of personal identity. Cartesian dualism entails that the real you is your soul, with your body being merely a non-essential vehicle that you walk around in, as it were. As complete substances, the soul can exist entirely apart from the body and (more to the present point) the body can exist entirely apart from the soul. This raises the puzzle of how you could know, even in principle, that in dealing with another person you are dealing with the *same* person over time. For all you ever observe is the person's body; you never observe, and never could observe, the person's soul, which is the thing that really *is* the person. So how do you know that the same soul, and thus the same person, is present in the body you're talking to now as was present in it last week or last year? Even if the personality traits and the like seem the same, that might just be because another soul is occupying the same body and pretending to be the original one. You could never know for sure – again, not even in principle, it seems. This "re-identification problem" is as stark a problem for Cartesian dualism as the interaction problem. But if we return to the hylemorphic conception of the soul as the form of the body, the problem disappears. For since matter is not, on that view, a complete substance in its own right, there simply cannot be matter without form, and thus cannot be a body without a soul. In particular, since your soul is the form of your body specific-ally, it follows that if your body is present, your soul is too, and thus you are present. The re-identification problem cannot arise.

A fourth and related advantage of Aquinas's hylemorphic dualism is that it provides a solution to the philosophical "problem of other minds." Given that all you ever observe is someone's body and behavior, and never observe nor could observe his or her thoughts and experiences, how do you know the latter even exist in the first place? How do you know the person isn't what philosophers call a "zombie" – a creature which is physically and behaviorally like a normal person down to the last detail, but which is totally devoid of consciousness? This is yet another problem that arises precisely because of the "mechanistic" conception of matter as inherently devoid of any sensory qualities or formal or final causes, which makes it seem possible that a living human body could exist without "qualia" and/or intentionality. But it is another problem which disappears if we look at things from a hylemorphic point of view. Again, a human body *just couldn't. be* a human body in the first place unless it had the form of a human body, and thus a rational soul, and thus sensation, intellect, and all the rest. So, "zombies" are metaphysically impossible, and you know that other people have minds *precisely because* they are physically and behaviorally identical to normal human beings.

There are further advantages to a hylemorphic approach to the philosophy of mind, some of which are discussed in my book *Philosophy of Mind*, cited above. But what has been said already suffices to show that Aquinas's view has, in addition to its intrinsic plausibility as a consequence of a general Aristotelian metaphysics (which, as I argued in chapter 2, is as defensible today as it ever was), a great deal of explanatory power with respect to problems of interest to contemporary philosophers of mind. Ironically enough, even some materialists have seen value in Aristotelian hylemorphism, though only because they have misinterpreted it as a variant of "functionalism." So that the Aristotelian–Thomistic position is not misunderstood, let us end this chapter by briefly noting some of the differences between the views in question.

Functionalism is a version of materialism according to which a mental state (such as a belief that it is raining outside, a sensation of pain, or whatever) should be analyzed in terms of its causal relations to stimulation of the sense organs, other mental states, and bodily behavior. So, for example, a sensation of pain is on this view to be analyzed as whatever internal state (of the brain, say) tends to be caused by damage to the body, tends also to produce such behaviors as screaming and crying, and does so in conjunction with other mental states which (by virtue of their own distinctive causal relations) can be identified as distress, annoyance, and the like. The idea is that what makes a mental state the kind of thing it is is the causal role it plays, not the kind of physical stuff the creature who has it is made out of. Hence, according to functionalism, if a robot were put together in such a way that the computer chips and wiring (or whatever) that made up its artificial "brain" functioned in a manner that paralleled the way neurons do, for example by sending signals between themselves in response to damage to the robot's body in such a way as to cause it to scream and cry, and so on, then the robot would literally experience pain just as we do, and indeed would in general have thoughts and experiences of just the sort we have.

Now since functionalism holds that it is the way in which material components are "organized" that gives rise to mental states, some have suggested that it is comparable to the Aristotelian hylemorphist idea that what makes certain parcels of matter living things capable of sensory and intellectual activity is the form that that matter has taken on. But the comparison is superficial. The crucial difference is that, like other forms of materialism, functionalism is implicitly committed to a "mechanistic" conception of the material world on which it is devoid of Aristotelian formal and final causes. For materialists, including functionalists, matter is not (as it is for Aristotelians and Thomists) essentially correlative with form, as that which has the potency to take on form, the "material cause" as opposed to the "formal cause" of a thing. Nor for them do material things have any inherent inclination to an end. Nor is quantity merely one category among others in terms of which we can describe the material world. Rather, matter is essentially and (depending on the extent of a given materialist's reductionism) even exhaustively describable in the mathematically quantifiable terms of modern physics, and material objects are causally related to one another only by way of (a thinly conceived version of) efficient cause.

Thus, by "functional organization," what the functionalist has in mind is the contingent arrangement of metaphysically independent material components according to certain regular patterns of efficient causation. A material thing is "nothing but" a collection of parts related in such a way. The difference from the Aristotelian notion of form could not be starker. For the hylemorphist, material things, including animals and people, are *irreducible* to their component parts; again, though a material thing can be analyzed as a composite of matter and form and an animal as a composite of soul and body, matter, form, soul, and body can themselves only be understood in terms of the wholes of which they are parts. The whole is also ordered to a certain natural end or final cause, and the various parts are themselves ordered to various ends that are subordinate to this overarching final cause. Accordingly, the parts are related by final causality as much as by efficient causality; and the unity between the parts is therefore *organic* and *necessary*, not "mechanical" and contingent. As we have seen, for the Aristotelian, a machine could not possibly count as a living thing, precisely because it is an artificial construct whose parts are *naturally* ordered to various other ends, rather than to the flourishing of the system into which they have been configured for human (and thus *external*) purposes. For the same reason, and contrary to the central thrust of functionalism, the Aristotelian–Thomistic hylemorphist would hold that it is metaphysically impossible for a robot, a computer, or any other artifact to be conscious or intelligent. For consciousness and intelligence as they exist in the material world are attributes of certain kinds of animals, animals are a certain kind of natural substance, and (to repeat) by definition an artifact, however complex, is not a natural substance, and thus of necessity cannot be living, or an animal, or conscious, or intelligent.

Finally, Aquinas thinks of the form of the human body as subsistent and thus immaterial; and the immateriality of the intellect (if not necessarily its subsistence) was something that Aristotle also affirmed. For this reason alone, their conception of "form" is quite obviously very different from anything the functionalist could accept. If their views are properly understood, Aristotle, Aquinas, and other hylemorphists would never be invited into the functionalist club. Nor would they want to join it.

5
Ethics

Throughout this book, I have emphasized how crucial a grasp of Aquinas's general metaphysics is to a proper understanding of his views in specific philosophical sub-disciplines such as the philosophy of religion and the philosophy of mind. It is no less crucial to understanding his views in that field which to contemporary philosophers might seem the furthest removed from metaphysics, namely ethics. Many philosophers today would heartily endorse Hilary Putnam's recent advocacy of what he calls "ethics without ontology." John Rawls famously defended a conception of justice he described as "political not metaphysical." It is widely assumed that the analysis and justification of fundamental moral claims can be conducted without reference to at least the more contentious issues of metaphysics. Nothing could be further from the spirit of Aquinas, for whom natural law (as his conception of morality is famously known) is "natural" precisely because it derives from human nature, conceived of in Aristotelian essentialist terms.

To be sure, recent decades have seen a tendency to try to reinterpret Aquinas's ethics in a way that divorces it from his now highly controversial essentialism. The most influential version of this approach is the "new natural law theory" of Germain Grisez and John Finnis. For Aquinas himself, however, and for Thomism historically, such a flight from Aristotelian metaphysics is neither necessary nor desirable. The truth about human beings can only be seen in light of the truth about the world in general. Aristotelian essentialism is not merely an abstract metaphysics but (as Henry Veatch has described it) an "ontology of morals."

The good

Now philosophers like Kai Nielsen and D. J. O'Connor have objected that Aquinas's metaphysical approach to ethics is a non-starter, on the grounds that it ignores the "fact/value distinction." For as Hume famously argued, conclusions about what *ought* to be done (which are statements about "value") cannot be inferred from premises concerning what *is* the case (statements of "fact"). To assume otherwise, it is claimed, is to commit the "naturalistic fallacy." The hope of side-stepping this objection to Aquinas is part of the reason why Grisez and Finnis have sought to develop a "new" natural law theory which, unlike the traditional version, does not seek to ground morality in factual premises concerning the metaphysics of human nature.

From the traditional Thomistic point of view, however, there simply is no "fact/value distinction" in the first place. More precisely, there is no such thing as a purely "factual" description of reality utterly divorced from "value," for "value" is built into the structure of the "facts" from the get-go. A gap between "fact" and "value" could exist only given a mechanistic-cum-nominalistic understanding of nature of the sort commonly taken for granted by modern philosophers, on which the world is devoid of any objective essences or natural ends. No such gap, and thus no "fallacy" of inferring normative conclusions from "purely factual" premises, can exist given an Aristotelian–Thomistic essentialist and teleological conception of the world. "Value" is a highly misleading term in any case, and subtly begs the question against critics of the "fact/value distinction" by insinuating that morality is purely subjective, insofar as "value" seems to presuppose someone doing the valuing. Aristotelians and Thomists (and other classical philosophers such as Platonists) tend to speak, not of "value," but of "the good," which on their account is entirely objective.

We have already seen how this is so, in our discussion of the convertibility of the transcendentals *being* and *good* in chapter 2. To return to a simple example from that discussion, it is of the essence of a triangle to be a closed plane figure with three straight sides, and anything with this essence must have a number of properties, such as having angles adding up to 180 degrees. These are straightforward objective facts, and remain so even though there are triangles which fail perfectly to match this description. A triangle drawn hastily on the cracked plastic seat of a moving bus might fail to have sides that are perfectly straight, and thus its angles will add up to something other than 180 degrees. Even a triangle drawn slowly and carefully on art paper with a straight edge and a Rapidograph pen will contain subtle flaws. Still, the latter will more perfectly approximate the essence of triangularity than the former will. It will be a *better* triangle than the former one. Indeed, we would naturally call the former a *bad* triangle and the latter a *good* one. This judgment would be completely objective; it would be silly to suggest that it reflects nothing more than a subjective preference for triangles with angles adding up to 180 degrees. It would be equally silly to suggest that we have somehow committed a fallacy in making a "value" judgment about the badness of the triangle drawn on the bus seat on the basis of the "facts" about the essence of triangularity. Given that essence, the "value judgment" in question obviously follows *necessarily*. This example illustrates how an entity can count as an instance of a certain kind of thing even if it fails perfectly to instantiate the essence of that kind of thing; a badly drawn triangle is not a non-triangle but a defective triangle. It also illustrates how there can be a perfectly *objective*, *factual* standard of goodness and badness, better and worse. To be sure, the standard in question in the current example is not a standard of *moral* goodness. But from an Aristotelian–Thomistic point of view, it illustrates a general notion of goodness of which moral goodness is a special case.

Livings things provide examples that bring us closer to a distinctively moral conception of goodness, as has been noted by several contemporary philosophers who, though not Thomists, have defended a kind of neo-Aristotelian position in ethics. For instance, Philippa Foot, following Michael Thompson, has noted how living things can only adequately be described in terms of what Thompson calls "Aristotelian categoricals" of a form such as S's are F, where S refers to a species and F to something predicated of the species. "Rabbits are herbivores," "Cats are four legged," and "Human beings have thirty-two teeth" would be instances of this general form. Note that such propositions cannot be adequately represented as either existential or universal propositions, as these are typically understood by modern logicians. "Cats are four legged," for instance, is not saying "There is at least one cat that is four legged"; it is obviously meant instead as a statement about cats in general. But neither is it saying "For everything that is a cat, it is four legged," since the occasional cat may be missing a leg due to injury or genetic defect. Aristotelian categoricals convey a *norm*, much like the description given above of what counts as a triangle. Any particular living thing can only be described as an instance of a species, and a species itself can only be described in terms of Aristotelian categoricals stating at least its general characteristics. If a particular S happens not to be F – if for example a certain cat is missing a leg – that does not show that S's are not F after all, but rather that this particular S is a *defective* instance of an S.

In living things the sort of norm in question is, as Foot also notes, inextricably tied to the notion of teleology; as Aquinas puts it, "all who rightly define *good* put in its notion something about its status as an end" (*QDV* 21.1). There are certain ends that any organism must realize in order to flourish as the kind of organism it is, ends concerning activities like self-maintenance, development, reproduction, the rearing of young, and so forth; and these ends entail a standard of goodness. Hence an oak that develops long and deep roots is to that extent a good oak and one that develops weak roots is to that extent bad and defective; a lioness which nurtures her young is to that extent a good lioness and one that fails to do so is to that extent bad and defective; and so on. As with the triangle example, it would be silly to pretend that these judgments of goodness and badness are in any way subjective or reflective of mere human preferences, or that the inferences leading to them commit a "naturalistic fallacy." For they simply follow from the objective facts about what counts as a flourishing or sickly instance of the biological kind or nature in question, and in particular from an organism's realization or failure to realize the ends set for it by its nature. The facts in question are, as it were, *inherently laden* with "value" from the start. Or, to use Foot's more traditional (and less misleading) language, the goodness a flourishing instance of a natural kind exhibits is "natural goodness" – the goodness is there *in the nature of things*, and not in our subjective "value" judgments about them.

What is true of animals in general is true of human beings. Like the other, non-rational animals, we have various ends inherent in our nature, and these determine what is good for us. In particular, Aquinas tells us, "all those things to which man has a *natural inclination*, are naturally apprehended by reason as being good, and consequently as objects of pursuit, and their contraries as evil, and objects of avoidance" (*ST* I-II.94.2, emphasis added). It is important not to misunderstand the force of Aquinas's expression "natural inclination" here. By "inclination" he does not necessarily mean something consciously desired, and by "natural" he doesn't mean something psychologically deep-seated, or even, necessarily, something genetically determined. What he has in mind are rather the *final causes* or *natural teleology* of our various capacities. For this reason, Anthony Lisska has suggested translating Aquinas's *inclinatio* as "disposition." While this has its advantages, even it fails to make it clear that Aquinas is not interested in just any dispositions we might contingently happen to have, but rather in those that reflect nature's purposes for us. Of course, there is often a close correlation between what nature intends and what we desire. Nature wants us to eat so that we'll stay alive, and sure enough we tend to want to eat. Given that we are social animals, nature intends for us to avoid harming others, and for the most part we do want to avoid this. Given that we need to reproduce ourselves, nature intends for us to have sexual relations, and obviously most people are quite happy to do so. At the same time, there are people (such as anorexics and bulimics) who form very strong desires not to eat what they need to eat in order to survive and thrive; and at the other extreme there are people whose desire for food is excessive. Some people are not only occasionally prone to harm others, but are positively misanthropic or sociopathic. And where sex is concerned, people often strongly desire to indulge in behaviors (masturbation, contraception, homosexual acts, and so forth) that are in Aquinas's view contrary to nature's purposes insofar as they do not have a natural tendency to result in procreation. Desires are nature's way of prodding us to do what is good for us, but like everything else in the natural order, they are subject to various imperfections and distortions. Hence, though in general and for the most part our desires match up with nature's purposes, this is not true in every single case. Habituated vice, peer pressure, irrationality, mental illness, and the like can often deform our subjective desires so that they turn us away from what nature intends, and thus from what is good for us. Genetic defect might do the same; just as it causes deformities like clubfoot and polydactyly, so too might it generate psychological and behavioral deformities as well.

Here as elsewhere, it is crucial in understanding Aquinas's views that one keeps his general metaphysical positions always in mind. "Natural" for Aquinas does not mean merely "statistically common," "in accordance with the laws of physics," "having a genetic basis," or any other of the readings that a mechanistic view of nature might suggest. It has instead to do with the final causes inherent in a thing by virtue of its essence, and which it possesses whether or not it ever realizes them or consciously wants to realize them. What is genuinely good for someone, accordingly, may in principle be something he or she does not want, like children who refuse to eat their vegetables, or an addict convinced that it would be bad to stop taking drugs. For Aquinas, knowing what is truly good for us requires taking an external, objective, "third-person" point of view on ourselves rather than a subjective "first-person" view; it is a matter of determining what fulfills our *nature*, not our contingent desires. The good in question has *moral* significance for us because, unlike other animals, we are capable of intellectually grasping what is good and freely choosing whether or not to pursue it.

Aquinas identifies three general categories of goods inherent in our nature. First are those we share in common with all living things, such as the preservation of our existence. Second are those common to animals specifically, such as sexual intercourse and the child-rearing activities that naturally follow upon it. Third are those peculiar to us as *rational* animals, such as "to know the truth about God, and to live in society," "to shun ignorance," and "to avoid offending those among whom one has to live" (*ST* I-II.94.2). These goods are ordered in a hierarchy corresponding to the hierarchy of living things (i.e. those with vegetative, sensory, and rational souls respectively). The higher goods presuppose the lower ones; for example, one cannot pursue truth if one is not able to conserve oneself in existence. But the lower goods are subordinate to the higher ones in the sense that they exist for the sake of the higher ones. The point of fulfilling the vegetative and sensory aspects of our nature is, ultimately, to allow us to fulfill the defining rational aspect of our nature.

What specifically will fulfill that nature? Or in other words, in what does the good for us, and thus our well-being or happiness, ultimately consist? It cannot be wealth, because wealth exists only for the sake of something else which we might acquire with it (*ST* I-II.2.1). It cannot be honor, because honor accrues to someone only as a consequence of realizing some good, and thus cannot itself be an ultimate good (*ST* I-II.2.2). For similar reasons, it cannot be fame or glory either, which are in any case often achieved for things that are not really good in the first place (*ST* I-II.2.3). Nor can it be power, for power is a means rather than an end and might be used to bring about evil rather than genuine good (*ST* I-II.2.4). It cannot be pleasure, because pleasure is also a consequence of realizing a good rather than the realization of a good itself; even less likely is it to be bodily pleasure specifically, since the body exists for the sake of the soul, which is immaterial (*ST* I-II.2.6). For the same reason, it cannot consist of any bodily good of any other sort (*ST* I-II.2.5). But neither can even it be a good of the soul, since the soul, as a created thing, exists for the sake of something else (i.e. that which creates it) (*ST* I-II.2.7). Obviously, then, it cannot be found in any created thing whatsoever; our *ultimate* end could only possibly be something "which lulls the appetite altogether," beyond which nothing more could be desired, and thus something absolutely *perfect* (*ST* I-II.2.8). And "this is to be found," Aquinas concludes, "not in any creature, but in God alone ... Wherefore God alone can satisfy the will of man ... God alone constitutes man's happiness" (*ST* I-II.2.8). That is not to deny that wealth, honor, fame, power, pleasure, and the goods of body and soul have their place; they cannot fail to do so given that we are the kinds of creatures that we are. Aquinas's point is that it is impossible for them to be the *highest* or *ultimate* good for us, that to which every other good is subordinated. God alone can be that.

In Aquinas's view, what is good for us is, as I have said, something that remains good for us even if for some reason we do not recognize it as good. What is good for us is *necessarily* good for us because it follows from our *nature*. As such, even God couldn't change it, any more than he could make two and two equal to five. Here we see one important consequence of Aquinas's view that the intellect is metaphysically prior to the will, in the sense that (as we saw in the last chapter) will derives from intellect rather than vice versa. The divine intellect knows the natures of things and the divine will creates in accordance with this knowledge. To be sure, the natures in question exist at first only as ideas in the divine mind itself; in this sense they are, like everything else, dependent on God. Still, in creating the things that are to have these natures, the divine will only ever creates in light of the divine ideas and never in a way that conflicts with what is possible given the content of those ideas. Aquinas's position is thus very far from the sort of "divine command ethics" according to which what is good is good *merely* because God wills it, so that absolutely anything (including torturing babies for fun, say) could have been good for us had he willed us to do it. This sort of view was famously taken by William of Ockham (c. 1287–1347), according to whom God could even have willed for us to hate him, in which case that is what would have been good for us. Such a position naturally follows from the "voluntarism" or emphasis on will over intellect associated with Ockham and John Duns Scotus (c. 1266–1308), which is one of the key features distinguishing their brands of Scholasticism from Thomism.

This difference between Aquinas and the voluntarists is related to the reasons for which Aquinas's position is, as we saw in chapter 3, immune to the famous "Euthyphro objection" to religiously based systems of ethics. The objection, it will be recalled, is in the form of a dilemma: either God wills something because it is good or it is good because he wills it; but if the former is true, then, contrary to theism, there will be something that exists independently of God (namely the standard of goodness he abides by in willing us to do something), and if the latter is true, then if God had willed us to torture babies for fun (say) then that would have been good, which seems obviously absurd. Ockham essentially takes the second horn of the dilemma, but for Aquinas the dilemma is a false one. What is good for us is good because of our nature and not because of some arbitrary divine command, and God only ever wills for us to do what is consistent with our nature. But that doesn't make the standard according to which he wills something existing independently of him, because what determines that standard are the ideas existing in the divine mind. Thus there is a third option between the two set out by the Euthyphro dilemma, and it is one that is neither inconsistent with our basic moral intuitions nor incompatible with the claims of theism.

Natural law

It is but a few short steps from "natural goodness" (as Foot calls it) to Aquinas's conception of natural law. The first principle of natural law, as Aquinas famously held, is that "*good is to be done and pursued, and evil is to be avoided*. All other precepts of the natural law are based upon this," where the content of those precepts is determined by the goods falling under the three main categories mentioned above (*ST* I-II.94.2). That "good is to be done" and so on might seem at first glance to be a difficult claim to justify, and certainly not a very promising candidate for a first principle. For isn't the question "Why should we be good?" precisely (part of) what any moral theory ought to answer? And isn't this question notoriously hard to answer to the satisfaction of moral skeptics?

Properly understood, however, Aquinas's principle is not only not difficult to justify, but even seems obviously correct. He is not saying that it is just self-evident that we ought to be morally good. Rather, he is saying that it is self-evident that whenever we act, we pursue something that we take to be good in some way and/or avoid what we take in some way to be evil or bad. And that seems clearly right. Even someone who does something he believes to be morally bad does so only because he is seeking something he regards as good in the sense of worth pursuing. Hence the mugger who admits that robbery is evil nevertheless takes his victim's wallet because he thinks it would be good to have money to pay for his drugs; hence the drug addict who regards his habit as wrong and degrading nevertheless thinks it would be good to satisfy his craving and bad to suffer the unpleasantness of not satisfying it. Of course, these claims are true only on a very thin sense of "good," but that is exactly the sense Aquinas intends.

Acceptance of Aquinas's general metaphysics is not necessary in order to see that this first principle is correct; it is supposed to be self-evident. But that metaphysics is meant to help us understand *why* it is correct. Like every other natural phenomenon, practical reason has a natural end or goal towards which it is ordered, and that end or goal is just whatever the intellect perceives to be good or worth pursuing. This claim too seems obvious, at least if one accepts Aquinas's Aristotelian metaphysics. And it brings us to the threshold of a further conclusion that does have real moral significance. Given what was said earlier, human beings, like everything else in the world, have various capacities and ends the fulfillment of which is good for them and the frustrating of which is bad, as a matter of objective fact. A rational intellect apprised of the facts will therefore perceive that it is good to realize these ends and bad to frustrate them. It follows, then, that a rational person will pursue the realization of these ends and avoid their frustration. In short, Aquinas's position is essentially this: practical reason is directed by nature towards the pursuit of what the intellect perceives as good; what is *in fact* good is the realization or fulfillment of the various ends inherent in human nature; and thus a *rational* person will perceive this and, accordingly, direct his or her actions towards the realization or fulfillment of those ends. In this sense, good action is just that which is "in accord with reason" (*ST* I-II.21.1; cf. *ST* I-II.90.1), and the moral skeptic's question "Why should I do what is good?" has an obvious answer: because to be rational *just is* (in part) to do what is good, to fulfill the ends set for us by nature. Natural law ethics as a body of substantive moral theory is the formulation of general moral principles on the basis of an analysis of these various human capacities and ends and the systematic working out of their implications. So, to take just one example, when we consider that human beings have intellects and that the natural end or function of the intellect is to grasp the truth about things, it follows that it is good for us – it fulfills our nature – to pursue truth and avoid error. Consequently, a rational person apprised of the facts about human nature will see that this is what is good for us and thus strive to attain truth and to avoid error. And so on for other natural human capacities.

Now things are bound to get more complicated than that summary perhaps lets on. Various qualifications and complications would need to be spelled out as the natural human capacities and ends are examined in detail, and not every principle of morality that follows from this analysis will necessarily be as simple and straightforward as "Pursue truth and avoid error." Particularly controversial among contemporary readers will be Aquinas's application of his method to questions of sexual morality (*SCG* III.122–126; *ST* II-II.151–154). Famously, he holds that the only sexual acts that can be morally justified are those having an inherent tendency towards procreation, and only when performed within marriage. The reason is that the natural *end* of sex is procreation, and because this includes not merely the generation of new human beings but also their upbringing, moral training and the like, which is a long-term project involving (in the normal case, for Aquinas) many children, a stable family unit is required in order for this end to be realized. Any other sexual behavior involves turning our natural capacities away from the end set for them by nature, and thus in Aquinas's view cannot possibly be good for us or rational. This rules out, among other things, masturbation, contraception, fornication, adultery, and homosexual acts.

This is a large topic which cannot be treated adequately here. (I discuss Aquinas's approach to sexual morality in detail in my book *The Last Superstition*.) But this much is enough to provide at least a general idea of how his natural law approach to ethics determines the specific content of our moral obligations. The *method* should be clear enough, whether or not one agrees with Aquinas's *application* of that method in any particular case. What has been said also suffices to give us a sense of the grounds of moral obligation, that which makes it the case that moral imperatives have categorical rather than merely hypothetical force (to use the distinction made famous by Kant). The hypothetical imperative (1) *If I want what is good for me then I ought to pursue what realizes my natural ends and avoid what frustrates them* is something whose truth Aquinas takes to follow from the metaphysical analysis of goodness sketched above. By itself, it does not give us a categorical imperative because the consequent will have force only for someone who accepts the antecedent. But that (2) *I do want what is good for me* is true of all of us by virtue of our nature as human beings, and is in Aquinas's view self-evident in any case, being just a variation on his fundamental principle of natural law. These premises yield the conclusion (3) *I ought to pursue what realizes my natural ends and avoid what frustrates them*. It does have categorical force because (2) has categorical force, and (2) has categorical force because it cannot be otherwise given our nature. Not only the content of our moral obligations but their obligatory character are thus determined, on Aquinas's analysis, by the metaphysics of final causality or natural teleology. As the neo-Scholastic natural law theorist Michael Cronin has summed up the Thomistic view, "In the fullest sense of the word, then, moral duty is natural. For not only are certain objects natural means to man's final end, but our desire of that end is natural also, and therefore, the necessity [or obligatory force] of the means is natural" (*Science of Ethics, Volume 1*, p. 222).

Clearly, the "naturalness" of natural law can, as I have emphasized, only be understood in terms of the Aristotelian metaphysics to which Aquinas is committed. But it is also illuminating to compare the natural law to the three other kinds of law distinguished by Aquinas. Most fundamental is what he calls the "eternal law," which is essentially the order of archetypes or ideas in the divine mind according to which God creates and providentially governs the world (*ST* I-II.91.1). Once the world, including human beings, is created in accordance with this law, the result is a natural order that human beings as rational animals can come to know and freely choose to act in line with, and "this participation of the eternal law in the rational creature is called the natural law" (*ST* I-II.91.2). The "natural law," then, can also be understood in terms of its contrast with eternal law, as the manifestation of the latter within the natural order. Now the natural law provides us with general principles by which individuals and societies ought to be governed, but there are many contingent and concrete details of human life that the natural law does not directly address. To take a standard example, the institution of private property is something we seem suited to given our nature, but there are many forms that institution might take consistent with natural law (cf. *ST* II-II.66.2). This brings us to "human law," which is the set of conventional or man-made principles that govern actual human societies, and which gives a "more particular determination" to the general requirements of the natural law as it is applied to concrete cultural and historical circumstances (*ST*

I–II.91.3). Human law, then, is unlike both eternal law and natural law in that it is "devised by human reason" and contingent rather than necessary and unchanging. Finally there is "divine law," which is law given directly by God, such as the Ten Commandments (*ST* I–II.91.4–5). This differs from the natural law in being knowable, not through an investigation of the natural order, but only via a divine revelation. It is like human law in being sometimes suited to contingent historical circumstances and thus temporary (as, in Aquinas's view, the Old Law given through Moses was superseded by the New Law given through Christ) but unlike human law in being infallible and absolutely binding.

Religion and morality

This naturally brings us to the question of the extent to which morality depends, in Aquinas's view, on religion in general and on an appeal to God's will in particular. Some of what has been said thus far might seem to imply that there is no such dependence, insofar as the content and binding force of the natural law have been said to derive from human nature rather than arbitrary divine commands. On the other hand, the idea that natural law derives from eternal law might seem to indicate that morality ultimately depends on God after all, as does the notion that only God (rather than wealth, pleasure, power, etc.) could be the ultimate good for us. So what is Aquinas's position?

Fulvio Di Blasi has usefully distinguished three approaches commentators have taken to the question of whether natural law, as understood in Thomistic terms, requires something like an Aristotelian metaphysical conception of the natural order and/or an appeal to theological premises concerning the existence and will of God. The first approach, associated with Grisez and Finnis, holds that natural law requires neither the metaphysics nor the theology. A second approach, represented by writers like Henry Veatch and Anthony Lisska, holds that the metaphysics is necessary but not the theology. The third approach holds that both elements are necessary, and is defended by commentators like Ralph McInerny and Di Blasi himself. As has been suggested already, the Grisez–Finnis approach to natural law seems clearly mistaken, at least if intended as an interpretation of Aquinas's own position. (Its value as a completely independent moral theory is something we cannot address here.) What of the other two approaches? It seems to me there is truth in both of them.

From an Aristotelian point of view, the essences and final causes of things are knowable simply by studying the things themselves, without any appeal to the existence or intentions of a creator. (Indeed, though Aristotle himself thought that the existence of a divine unmoved mover could be proved, he did not, as Aquinas later would in his Fifth Way, try to argue that the *final causes* of things, specifically, required an explanation in theological terms. Aristotle's own arguments for God were variants of what Aquinas called the First Way.) But at least the core of the theory of natural law follows directly from these metaphysical notions. Hence it seems clear that at least a substantial part of morality can, on a Thomistic account, be known in principle without appealing to God. If we know that the will is naturally ordered to pursuing what the intellect perceives as good, and know that what is in fact good is what realizes our natural ends, then we can know that if we are rational we ought to pursue those ends. Moreover, since those ends can themselves be known through reason, we can arrive at some knowledge of what it is specifically that the natural law requires of us even if we have no knowledge of God. To be sure, if Aquinas is right that God alone can be our *ultimate* end, then without knowledge of this fact, our understanding of morality will be deficient, to say the least. Still, we would nevertheless have some substantial understanding of it. And while if there is a God he will, of

course, be the ultimate explanation of the natural law (since he
will be the ultimate explanation of *everything*), lack of knowledge
of God wouldn't prevent us from knowing something about the
natural law, any more than it would prevent us from discovering various scientific truths.

So there is some truth to the view defended by Veatch and
Lisska. On the other hand, it seems highly implausible to suggest
that the existence of God, as Aquinas understands him, could
possibly be irrelevant to a Thomistic understanding of natural
law. For if God exists, then he cannot fail to be our ultimate end,
in which case everything else in our moral lives would necessarily have to be subordinated to our religious obligations; and even
the most conservative form of secular life cannot fail to be
altered radically when redirected towards a religious end. Hence
if God exists an adequate account of the *content* of morality will
necessarily have to reflect this fact.

Our understanding of the grounds of moral *obligation* is also
bound to be affected by theological considerations. Indeed,
Aquinas takes the view that in the strict sense, "law ... is nothing
else than an ordinance of reason for the common good, made by
him who has care of the community, and promulgated" (*ST* I-
II.90.4). Like every other form of law, then, the natural law, if
it is truly to count as *law* (rather than a mere counsel of
prudence) must be backed by a *lawgiver*. Since it is a law govern-
ing the natural order, the lawgiver in question would just be the
source of the natural order, namely God, who promulgates the
natural law "by the very fact that God instilled it into man's
mind so as to be known by him naturally" (*ST* I-II.90.4).

Aquinas's view seems to be that since things are *fully* intelligible only when traced back to the creative will of God – who,
as pure act, cause of all things, the one absolutely necessary
being, perfect goodness, and the supreme intellect, can alone
serve as an ultimate explanation of anything – the necessity or
obligatory nature of our moral obligations too can also only be

fully intelligible when traced back to him. For a rational agent will act only in accordance with what reason and nature command, and precisely because reason and nature command it. But reason and nature only command what they do because God has ordered them that way. Hence a rational agent cognizant of the ultimate source of things will act only in accordance with what the divine will commands, and precisely because the divine will commands it:

> In this way God Himself is the measure of all beings ... Hence His intellect is the measure of all knowledge; His goodness, of all goodness; and, to speak more to the point, His good will, of every good will. Every good will is therefore good by reason of its being conformed to the divine good will. Accordingly, since everyone is obliged to have a good will, he is likewise obliged to have a will conformed to the divine will. (*QDV* 23.7)

Thus there is, from the Thomistic point of view, some truth after all in the "divine command" theory of ethics, even if it is far from the whole story and even though the commands in question are emphatically not arbitrary ones.

More to the present point, there is much truth in Di Blasi's view that Aquinas's theory of natural law is ultimately as theological as it is metaphysical. But the "ultimately" is important. As Michael Cronin notes, and as we have seen when discussing the Five Ways,

> the eternal law of God does not move the world directly and immediately, but mediately, *i.e.*, through the operation of secondary causes or causes residing in nature itself; and therefore it is not to be expected that in the moral world the eternal law will be operative without some such intermediate natural principle. (*Science of Ethics*, vol. 1, p. 213)

Hence while what Cronin calls the "ultimate ground" of moral obligation is "eternal law of the Supreme Lawgiver," there is also "a proximate ground of duty residing in nature itself," namely the fact that the will is unalterably fixed by nature on the pursuit of the good as its natural end or final cause. And this proximate ground can be studied independently of the ultimate ground, just as the secondary causes of things can be studied without reference to the First Cause. While the Grisez–Finnis reading of Aquinas seems simply mistaken, then, the Veatch–Lisska reading is not mistaken so much as incomplete. A natural law theory with Aristotelian metaphysics but without God is not false, even if it isn't the whole truth either. It is, we might say, a study of the "proximate grounds" of morality, just as natural science is the study of the proximate or secondary causes of observed phenomena. Still, in morality as in science, a *complete* account must necessarily be a theological one.

In both its metaphysical and its theological commitments, Aquinas's system of ethics is, like the rest of his philosophy, obviously radically at odds with the assumptions typically made by contemporary moral philosophers. But the main difference may lie in something other than a disagreement over this or that particular ontological thesis or argument for God's existence, in basic ethos rather than intellectual orientation. The spirit of modern moral philosophy is perhaps summed up best in Kant's famous characterization of human beings as "ends in themselves" and "self-legislators." This sort of talk would sound blasphemous and even mad to Aquinas, for whom God alone, as the "first cause and last end of all things," could possibly be said to be the source of moral law and an end in himself (*ST* I-II.62.1, as translated by Pegis in *Basic Writings of Saint Thomas Aquinas*). For Aquinas, we are not here for ourselves, but for the glory of God, and precisely because this is the end set for us by nature, it is in him alone that we can find our true happiness. And it must be emphasized that, as with the other themes we've explored in this book, he takes this conclusion to be a matter, not of faith, but of *reason itself*.

Therein lies the sting of Aquinas's challenge to modernity.

Further reading

Chapter 1

G. K. Chesterton, *Saint Thomas Aquinas* (Doubleday, 1956) is an older popular introduction to Aquinas's life and work. More recent and scholarly is James Weisheipl, *Friar Thomas d'Aquino* (Doubleday, 1974). Most recent of all is Jean-Pierre Torrell, *Saint Thomas Aquinas, Volume 1: The Person and His Work*, revised edition (Catholic University of America Press, 2005).

General introductions to Aquinas's thought include: F. C. Copleston, *Aquinas* (Pelican Books, 1955); Brian Davies, *Aquinas* (Continuum, 2002); Brian Davies, *The Thought of Thomas Aquinas* (Oxford University Press, 1992); Etienne Gilson, *The Christian Philosophy of St. Thomas Aquinas* (Random House, 1956); Anthony Kenny, *Aquinas* (Oxford University Press, 1980); Herbert McCabe, *On Aquinas* (Continuum, 2008); Ralph McInerny, *Aquinas* (Polity Press, 2004); Ralph McInerny, *St. Thomas Aquinas* (University of Notre Dame Press, 1982); Robert Pasnau and Christopher Shields, *The Philosophy of Aquinas* (Westview, 2004); and Eleonore Stump, *Aquinas* (Routledge, 2003).

Useful collections of essays on Aquinas include: Brian Davies, ed., *Aquinas's Summa Theologiae: Critical Essays* (Rowman and Littlefield, 2006); Brian Davies, ed., *Thomas Aquinas: Contemporary Philosophical Perspectives* (Oxford University Press, 2002); Anthony Kenny, ed., *Aquinas: A Collection of Critical Essays* (Anchor Books, 1969); Fergus Kerr, ed., *Contemplating Aquinas* (SCM Press, 2003); and Norman Kretzmann and Eleonore Stump, eds., *The Cambridge Companion to Aquinas* (Cambridge University Press, 1993).

Chapter 2

The general works on Aquinas cited in the previous chapter all contain useful introductory discussions of his key metaphysical ideas. A brief survey can also be found in John Haldane, "A Thomist Metaphysics," in Richard Gale, ed., *The Blackwell Guide to Metaphysics* (Blackwell, 2002). A recent full-length general study can be found in John Wippel, *The Metaphysical Thought of Thomas Aquinas* (Catholic University of America Press, 2000).

Recent defenses of Aristotelian–Thomistic essentialism include Gyula Klima's "Contemporary Essentialism vs. Aristotelian Essentialism," in John Haldane, ed., *Mind, Metaphysics, and Value in the Thomistic and Analytic Traditions* (University of Notre Dame Press, 2002), and David Oderberg, *Real Essentialism* (Routledge, 2007). An introduction to "new essentialist" philosophy of science can be found in Brian Ellis, *The Philosophy of Nature* (Acumen, 2002). Nancy Cartwright's "Aristotelian Natures and the Modern Experimental Method" is in John Earman, ed., *Inference, Explanation, and Other Frustrations* (University of California Press, 1992). Crawford Elder's views are developed in *Real Natures and Familiar Objects* (M.I.T. Press, 2004), and George Molnar's in *Powers* (Oxford University Press, 2003).

I assess the early modern philosophers' anti-Scholastic arguments in more detail in *The Last Superstition: A Refutation of the New Atheism* (St. Augustine's Press, 2008) and in *Locke* (Oneworld Publications, 2007). The former work also includes a detailed case for the reality of final causes. Two important recent articles on final causality are John Hawthorne and Daniel Nolan, "What Would Teleological Causation Be?" in Hawthorne's *Metaphysical Essays* (Oxford University Press, 2006), and David Oderberg, "Teleology: Inorganic and Organic," in Ana Marta Gonzalez, ed., *Contemporary Perspectives on Natural Law* (Ashgate, 2008). Monte Ransome Johnson, *Aristotle on Teleology* (Oxford University Press, 2005) is an important book-length treatment. Paul Davies's remarks were quoted from *The Fifth Miracle* (Simon and Schuster, 1999), and Max Delbrück's remarks from his essay "Aristotle-totle-totle," in Jacques Monod and Ernest Borek, eds., *Of Microbes and Life* (Columbia University Press, 1971). The irreducibly teleological character of human action is discussed by G. F. Schueler in *Reasons and Purposes* (Oxford University Press, 2003) and by Scott Sehon in *Teleological Realism* (M.I.T. Press, 2005).

Anscombe's critique of Hume can be found in her articles "'Whatever has a Beginning of Existence must have a Cause': Hume's Argument Exposed," in her *Collected Philosophical Papers, Volume 1* (Basil Blackwell, 1981), and "Times, Beginnings and Causes," in her *Collected Philosophical Papers, Volume 2* (Basil Blackwell, 1981). Haldane's remarks are in his volume co-written with J. J. C. Smart, *Atheism and Theism*, second edition (Blackwell, 2003).

Anthony Kenny's critique of Aquinas can be found in *Aquinas on Being* (Oxford University Press, 2002) and in chapter 2 of *Aquinas*, cited at the end of the previous chapter (this is the work in which Kenny makes the "sophistry and illusion" remark). Brian Davies replies to Kenny in "Aquinas, God, and Being," *The Monist* 80 (1997); Gyula Klima, in "On Kenny on Aquinas on Being," *International Philosophical Quarterly* 44 (2004); and Barry Miller, in *A Most Unlikely God* (University of Notre Dame Press, 1996). David Braine's "Aquinas, God, and Being" and John Knasas's "Haldane's Analytic Thomism and Aquinas's *Actus Essendi*" are in Craig Paterson and Matthew Pugh, eds., *Analytical Thomism* (Ashgate, 2006). Knasas explores these issues at greater length in his *Being and Some Twentieth-Century Thomists* (Fordham University Press, 2003).

Chapter 3

Substantial discussion of the Five Ways can be found in: G. E. M. Anscombe and P. T. Geach, *Three Philosophers* (Basil Blackwell, 1961); Reginald Garrigou-Lagrange, *God: His Existence and His Nature* (in two volumes) (B. Herder, 1934); Etienne Gilson, *The*

Christian Philosophy of St. Thomas Aquinas (Random House, 1956); Maurice Holloway, *An Introduction to Natural Theology* (Appleton-Century-Crofts, 1959); G. H. Joyce, *Principles of Natural Theology* (Longmans, Green, and Co., 1924); Anthony Kenny, *The Five Ways* (Routledge and Kegan Paul, 1969); Jacques Maritain, *Approaches to God* (Macmillan, 1967); Christopher Martin, *Thomas Aquinas: God and Explanations* (Edinburgh University Press, 1997); R. P. Phillips, *Modern Thomistic Philosophy, Volume II* (Newman Press, 1950); Henri Renard, *The Philosophy of God* (Bruce Publishing Company, 1951); and John Wippel, *The Metaphysical Thought of Thomas Aquinas* (Catholic University of America Press, 2000).

The first three ways are often set apart in discussions of Aquinas's natural theology as versions of the cosmological argument for God's existence. Important discussions of one or more of these arguments can be found in: Celestine Bittle, *God and His Creatures* (Bruce Publishing Company, 1953); David Braine, *The Reality of Time and the Existence of God* (Oxford University Press, 1988); William Lane Craig, *The Cosmological Argument from Plato to Leibniz* (Harper and Row, 1980); Norman Kretzmann, *The Metaphysics of Theism* (Oxford University Press, 1997); J. L. Mackie, *The Miracle of Theism* (Oxford University Press, 1982); William Rowe, *The Cosmological Argument* (Fordham University Press, 1998); and J. J. C. Smart and J. J. Haldane, *Atheism and Theism*, second edition (Blackwell, 2003).

The argument from motion raises unique issues of its own, useful discussions of which can be found in: Michael Augros, "Ten Objections to the *Prima Via*," *Peripatetikos* 6 (2007); Scott MacDonald, "Aquinas's Parasitic Cosmological Argument," in *Medieval Philosophy and Theology*, Volume 1 (University of Notre Dame Press, 1991); Rudi te Velde, *Aquinas on God* (Ashgate, 2006); and William Wallace, "Newtonian Antinomies Against the *Prima Via*," *The Thomist* 19 (1956). The question of infinite causal regresses is addressed in: Patterson Brown, "Infinite Causal Regression," in Kenny, ed., *Aquinas: A Collection of Critical Essays*;

Stephen Davis, "Hierarchical Causes in the Cosmological Argument," *International Journal for Philosophy of Religion* 31 (1992); Barry Miller, "Necessarily Terminating Causal Series and the Contingency Argument," *Mind* XCI (1982); and James Sadowksy, "The Cosmological Argument and the Endless Regress," *International Philosophical Quarterly* 20 (1980).

Many of the works cited above contain substantial discussions of Aquinas's derivation of the divine attributes. Especially useful are volume 2 of Garrigou-Lagrange's *God: His Existence and His Nature* and Kretzmann's *The Metaphysics of Theism*. Also important are chapters 3–5 of Eleonore Stump, *Aquinas* (Routledge, 2003). Brian Davies, *The Reality of God and the Problem of Evil* (Continuum, 2006) is a detailed treatment of the problem of evil written from a Thomistic point of view. Christopher Hughes, *On a Complex Theory of a Simple God* (Cornell University Press, 1989) criticizes the idea of divine simplicity while Barry Miller, *A Most Unlikely God* (University of Notre Dame Press, 1996) defends it.

Chapter 4

Recent studies of Aquinas's psychology include: Anthony Kenny, *Aquinas on Mind* (Routledge, 1993); Norman Kretzmann, *The Metaphysics of Creation* (Oxford University Press, 1999), chapters 8–10; Robert Pasnau, *Thomas Aquinas on Human Nature* (Cambridge University Press, 2002); and Eleonore Stump, *Aquinas* (Routledge, 2003), Part II. Three useful articles are Gyula Klima, "Man = Body + Soul: Aquinas's Arithmetic of Human Nature," in Brian Davies, ed., *Thomas Aquinas: Contemporary Philosophical Perspectives* (Oxford University Press, 2002); Norman Kretzmann, "Philosophy of Mind," in Norman Kretzmann and Eleonore Stump, eds., *The Cambridge Companion to Aquinas* (Oxford University Press, 1993); and Herbert McCabe, "The Immortality of the Soul," in Anthony Kenny, ed., *Aquinas: A Collection of Critical Essays* (Anchor Books, 1969).

Recent works applying broadly Aristotelian and/or Thomistic arguments to issues in contemporary philosophy of mind include: David Braine, *The Human Person* (University of Notre Dame Press, 1992); John Haldane, "A Return to Form in the Philosophy of Mind," in David Oderberg, ed., *Form and Matter* (Blackwell, 1999); Brian Leftow, "Souls Dipped in Dust," in Kevin Corcoran, ed., *Soul, Body, and Survival* (Cornell University Press, 2001); John O'Callaghan, *Thomist Realism and the Linguistic Turn* (University of Notre Dame Press, 2003); David Oderberg, "Hylemorphic Dualism," in Ellen Frankel Paul, Fred D. Miller, Jr., and Jeffrey Paul, eds., *Personal Identity* (Cambridge University Press, 2005); and James Ross, "Immaterial Aspects of Thought," *Journal of Philosophy* 89 (1992). The Aristotelian–Thomistic analyses of life and biological species are defended in David Oderberg, *Real Essentialism* (Routledge, 2007), chapters 8 and 9.

For the debate over Aquinas and abortion, see Pasnau's *Thomas Aquinas on Human Nature*, chapter 4; John Haldane and Patrick Lee, "Aquinas on Human Ensoulment, Abortion, and the Value of Life," *Philosophy* 78, no. 2 (2003); Pasnau's "Souls and the Beginning of Life (A Reply to Haldane and Lee)," *Philosophy* 78, no. 4 (2003); and Haldane and Lee's "Rational Souls and the Beginning of Life (A Reply to Robert Pasnau)," *Philosophy* 78, no. 4 (2003).

Chapter 5

Recent works on Aquinas's ethics include: Fulvio Di Blasi, *God and the Natural Law* (St. Augustine's Press, 2006); Anthony Lisska, *Aquinas's Theory of Natural Law* (Oxford University Press, 1996); Ralph McInerny, *Aquinas on Human Action* (Catholic University of America Press, 1992); and Ralph McInerny, *Ethica Thomistica*, revised edition (Catholic University of America Press, 1997). John Goyette, Mark Latkovic, and Richard Myers, eds., *St. Thomas Aquinas and the Natural Law Tradition* (Catholic University of America Press, 2004) is a useful collection of essays.

The "new natural law theory" approach to Aquinas's ethics is developed in Germain Grisez, "The First Principle of Practical Reason," in Anthony Kenny, ed., *Aquinas: A Collection of Critical Essays* (Doubleday, 1969) and John Finnis, *Aquinas* (Oxford University Press, 1998). It is criticized briefly in the first edition of McInerny's *Ethica Thomistica* and in his *Aquinas on Human Action*, and at greater length in Lisska's *Aquinas's Theory of Natural Law* and in Henry Veatch, "Natural Law and the 'Is'–'Ought' Question: Queries to Finnis and Grisez," in *Swimming Against the Current in Contemporary Philosophy* (Catholic University of America Press, 1990).

Criticisms of Aquinas based on the "fact/value distinction" are presented by Kai Nielsen in *Philosophy and Atheism* (Prometheus Books, 1985), and by D. J. O'Connor in *Aquinas and Natural Law* (Macmillan, 1968). The distinction is criticized in Christopher Martin, "The Fact/Value Distinction," in David Oderberg and Timothy Chappell, eds., *Human Values* (Palgrave Macmillan, 2004). Also relevant is Peter Geach, "Good and Evil," in Philippa Foot, ed., *Theories of Ethics* (Oxford University Press, 1967).

For Foot's neo-Aristotelian approach to ethics, see *Natural Goodness* (Oxford: Clarendon Press, 2001). Michael Thompson's "The Representation of Life" is in Rosalind Hursthouse, Gavin Lawrence, and Warren Quinn, eds., *Virtues and Reasons* (Oxford: Clarendon Press, 1995). For a recent defense of the metaphysical underpinnings of Aquinas's natural law theory, see David Oderberg, "The Metaphysical Foundations of Natural Law," in H. Zaborowski, ed., *Natural Law and Contemporary Society* (Catholic University of America Press, forthcoming). Michael Cronin, *The Science of Ethics* (in two volumes) (M. H. Gill and Son, 1939) is an important older work which has informed my own understanding of the Thomistic account of moral obligation.

Index

abortion 138–142

act and potency 9–12, 19, 28–29, 31, 65–66, 68–69, 73, 75, 118, 132, 160

action 51, 167–8 *see also* will

Albert the Great 4, 63

analogy 32–33, 58, 105–7, 124, 128

angels 13, 15, 28–29, 31, 60, 96, 98, 105–6, 123

Anscombe, Elizabeth 53–54

Anselm 62, 127, 130

Appetite 124

Aristotelianism 4–6, 38–42, 44, 50, 103–4, 132, 134–40, 173, 174, 175, 177

Aristotle 4, 9, 47, 63, 137, 158, 159–60, 169, 189 *see also* Aristotelianism

artifacts 136–7, 173

Athanasius 127

Augustine 34, 63, 127

Augustinianism 5

Averroes 63, 127

Averroism 5

Avicenna 63, 127

Bacon, Francis 40

being 31–33, 105, 108 *see also* existence

Berkeley, George 144

Big Bang 64

Braine, David 58

Brown, Patterson 72

Burtt, E. A. 41–42

cannibal problem *see* resurrection

Cartesian dualism 131, 138–9, 163–4, 166, 167–8, 169–70

Cartwright, Nancy 49–50

causality, principle of 11, 22–23, 53–55, 64–65, 67–69, 81–82, 95, 114

causation *see* efficient cause, four causes

chance 113–15

change *see* motion

conceptualism 26

conservation, divine 85, 88

contingent vs. necessary 86–87, 90–93, 94–99

cosmological argument *see* First Way; Second Way; Third Way

Craig, William Lane 86–87

Cronin, Michael 187, 191–2

Darwinism *see* evolution

Davies, Brian 56–57, 125

Davies, Paul 46–47, 52
Dawkins, Richard 63–64, 104,
  105, 110
deism 111, 118
Delbrück, Max 47
Democritus 146
Descartes, Rene 37, 40, 51,
  131, 133, 138, 139, 161
design argument 64, 110–11,
  112, 113, 115, 118
Di Blasi, Fulvio 188–9, 191
divine attributes 63, 64, 66,
  120–30
divine command theory
  182–3, 188, 191 see also
  ethics, religion and;
  Euthyphro dilemma
divine law 188
DNA 45–47
dualism see Cartesian dualism;
  hylemorphic dualism;
  property dualism
Duns Scotus 182

efficient cause 16, 20–23,
  51–55, 102, 103, 108,
  163–4
  immanent vs. transeunt
  135–7
  per accidens vs. per se
  69–72, 83, 85, 88–89
  presupposes final cause 20,
  43, 44–51, 112–13, 114
  second causes 72, 191–2
Elder, Crawford 61
Ellis, Brian 50
empiricism 53, 144
essence and existence 24–31,

  55–61, 84–86, 97–98,
  108, 120–1, 159
essentialism 24–28, 50, 60–61,
  91, 108, 174
eternal law 187–8
ethics 128–9, 143, 174 see also
  goodness; natural law
  obligatory force of 186–7,
  190–2
  religion and 188–92 see also
  divine command theory
euthanasia 139–40
Euthyphro dilemma 128–9,
  182–3
evil 35–36, 124–6
evolution 44–45, 52–53, 110,
  112, 113, 115
exemplarity, principle of 102
existence 29–30, 55–59, 99,
  129
existential proof 84–88, 98,
  108

fact/value distinction 175–80
faith 2–3
Fifth Way 37, 64, 110–20, 189
final cause 16–19, 35, 36–51,
  149, 163, 165–6, 167–8,
  173
  and Fifth Way 110, 112–20
  and goodness 177–82,
  184–5, 186–7
  in living things 135, 142
finality, principle of 18, 23,
  114
Finnis, John 174, 175, 188–9,
  192
First Way 65–81, 149, 189

Five Ways 62–65, 110 *see also*
    First Way; Second Way;
    Third Way; Fourth Way;
    Fifth Way
Fodor, Jerry 45
Foot, Philippa 177–8, 183
form 13–14, 15, 16, 24, 92,
    102, 103, 132, 139, 148,
    153–5, 159–60
formal cause 16, 118, 163, 165
    see also form; substantial
    form
  and Fourth Way 102, 103,
    108
  soul as 166, 167–8
four causes 16–23
Fourth Way 99–109
freedom *see* will
Frege, Gottlob 33, 55–59, 128
function, biological 44–45
functionalism 171–3

Galileo 41
Garrigou-Lagrange, Reginald
    72, 74, 80, 113, 114, 118
Geach, Peter 56, 57, 88
Gilson, Etienne 44, 83
God 28, 34, 159, 182 *see also*
    First Way; Second Way;
    Third Way; Fourth Way;
    Fifth Way
  eternal 80, 122
  First Cause 55, 64–65, 109
    see also Second Way
  goodness of 124–6, 128–9
  immaterial 122
  immutable 122
  incorporeal 122

  intellect 123
  knowledge of 123, 157
  last end of human beings
    143, 181, 192
  morality and *see* divine
    command theory; ethics,
    religion and
  one 120–1
  perfection 124
  power of 123
  pure act 12, 30, 74–76, 105,
    109, 118, 121, 122, 124,
    157
  simplicity of 58, 99, 126–9
  subsistent existence 30,
    56–57, 84–86, 98, 99,
    109, 118, 120–1
  Supreme Intelligence *see*
    Fifth Way
  Unmoved Mover *see* First
    Way
  will of 123–4
God of the gaps 111, 112,
    157
goodness 33, 34–36, 106–7,
    124, 175–85
Grisez, Germain 174, 175,
    188–9, 192

Haldane, John 55, 141, 148
henological argument *see*
    Fourth Way
hierarchy of being 30–31,
    105–8, 138, 157
Holloway, Maurice 82
human law 187–8
Hume, David 20–22, 53–54,
    82, 88–89, 144, 175

hylemorphic dualism 162–73
  see also intellect,
  immateriality of; soul,
  immortality of
hylemorphism 13–16, 92, 96,
  97, 132, 160, 166, 167–8,
  173

imagination 53, 144, 145, 156
individuation, principle of
  27–28
induction 43
inertia 76–79
infinite regress 69–72, 83, 85,
  88–89, 109, 118
intellect 53, 107, 138, 140,
  142–9
  active vs. passive 145–6
  differs from imagination 53,
    144–5, 156
  immateriality of 123, 151–8
  relation to will 123–4, 143,
    149, 182
Intelligent Design theory 46,
  110, 111, 116, 119
intentionality 50–51, 131,
  147–9, 164, 165, 167, 170
interaction problem 164, 165,
  166, 167–8

John Damascene 63
Joyce, G. H. 80

Kant, Immanuel 82–83, 186,
  192
Kenny, Anthony 55–60, 65,
  68, 74, 160
Klima, Gyula 25, 57, 58, 61
Knasas, John 58–59
Kretzmann, Norman 76
Kripke, Saul 25, 61

laws, physical 48–51, 113
Lee, Patrick 141
Leibniz, G. W. 98
life 106–7, 132–8, 139, 173
Lisska, Anthony 178, 189, 192
Locke, John 26

MacDonald, Scott 74–76
MacIntyre, Alasdair 42
Mackie, J. L. 95, 98
Maimonides 63, 122, 127
Martin, Christopher F. J. 1–2,
  97, 100
material cause see matter; prime
  matter
materialism 131, 163, 164,
  166, 168, 171, 172
matter 13–14, 16, 27–28,
  92–93, 95–98, 132, 160,
  163–6, 168–9
McInerny, D. Q. 76
McInerny, Ralph 189
mechanistic view of nature
  39–43, 50–51, 64, 112,
  115, 132, 136–7
  and ethics 175
  and mind-body problem
    163–6, 168–9, 170, 172
mental causation 168 see also
  interaction problem
Miller, Barry 58

mind *see* intellect, soul
mind-body problem 131–2,
    165
Molière 37–38
Molnar, George 50
morality *see* ethics
motion 10, 65–66, 67–69, 73,
    75, 76–79

natural law 174, 183–92
naturalistic fallacy *see* fact/value
    distinction
necessary being *see* contingent
    vs. necessary
negative theology 57, 80, 122,
    130
Neoplatonism 5, 30
new natural law theory 174,
    175, 188–9
Newton, Isaac 76–79
Nielsen, Kai 175

O'Connor, D. J. 175
Oderberg, David 25, 47–48,
    61, 163
ontological argument 62, 130
ontology 31, 174
other minds, problem of 170–1

Paley, William 64, 110–11,
    112, 115, 118, 119
Parmenides 9–10
participation 102, 108–9
Pasnau, Robert 135, 141–2
perception 146–9
personal identity 169–70

Plato *see* Platonism
Platonism 15, 24, 26, 60,
    100–4, 108, 117, 146,
    159–60, 161, 175
possible worlds 11, 24–25,
    91–92, 96, 99
powers 38, 39, 49–50
practical reason 183–5
prime matter 14, 15, 97, 106
privation 36
properties 25–26, 129, 164
property dualism 131, 163,
    164–5, 166
proportionate causality,
    principle of 22–23,
    51–53, 68
Pseudo-Dionysius 122
Ptolemaic astronomy 39
Putnam, Hilary 25, 61, 174

qualia 131, 164–5, 168–9,
    170
quantum mechanics 54–55

Rawls, John 174
realism 15, 24, 26, 60, 103
reductionism 14–15, 172–3
relativism 103
Renard, Henri 102
resurrection 161–2
Ross, James 156–7

Scholasticism 37–42, 182
Schueler, G. F. 51
science 2, 38–42, 44–51,
    76–79

Searle, John 45
Second Way 64–65, 81–90,
    98, 108
Sehon, Scott 51
sensation 143–6
Sertillanges, A. D. 72
sexual morality 179, 185–6
Shields, Christopher 25, 135
simplicity, divine 58, 99,
    126–9
soul 15, 28, 31, 131, 132–42,
    166, 169–70
  animal or sensory 137–8,
    151
  ensoulment 138–42
  immortality of 125, 151,
    157–62
  rational or intellective 138,
    140, 151. 158
  vegetative or nutritive 137,
    151
Stump, Eleonore 128–9
substance 13, 15, 32, 97,
    105–6, 136–7, 160–1,
    163–4, 166
substantial form 13–14, 39, 97

teleological argument *see* Fifth
    Way
teleology *see* final cause
Third Way 86–87, 90–99

Thomism 6, 182
Thomistic dualism *see*
    hylemorphic dualism
Thompson, Michael 177
transcendentals 31–36, 104–5,
    106–7, 108–9, 176
truth 33–34
Twenty-Four Thomistic
    Theses 12

universals 15, 24, 26–27, 34,
    102, 144, 152, 155–7
Unmoved Mover *see* First Way

Veatch, Henry 174, 189, 192
Velde, Rudi te 68
vitalism 133
voluntarism 182

will 123–4, 138, 140, 142–3,
    149–51
  freedom of 149–51
  relation to intellect 123–4,
    143, 149, 182
William of Ockham 182, 183
Wippel, John 72, 105, 109

zombies 170–1

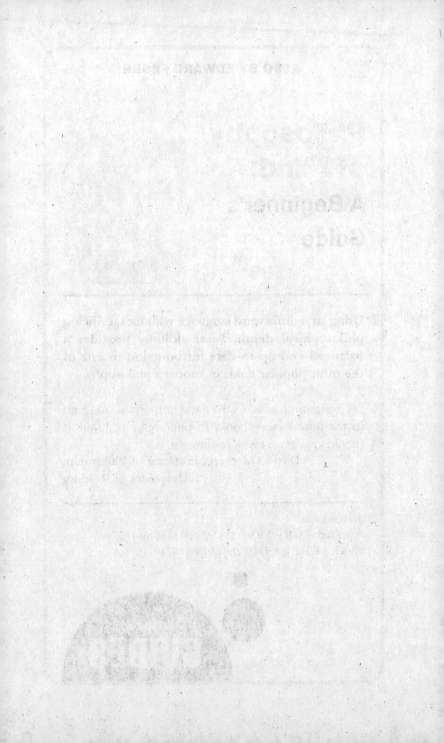